Utilizing Older for Competitive Advantage

The New Human Resources Frontier

Edited by William K. Zinke

Center for Productive Longevity
Boulder, Colorado

Copyright © 2008 by William K. Zinke
All rights reserved
Printed in the United States of America

No part of this publication may be reproduced, stored in, or introduced into a retrieval system, or transmitted, in any form, or by any means (electronic, mechanical, photocopying, recording, or otherwise), without the prior permission of the publisher.

Library of Congress Cataloging-in-Publication Data
Zinke, William, 1927-
    Utilizing older workers for competitive advantage: the new human resources frontier / William K. Zinke.
    p. cm.
    ISBN: 978-0-615-22234-9

1. Business 2. Management 3. Human Resources 4. Workflow Planning

First Printing, June 2008
Cover design and layout by Mona Simon
Editing by Dawn Peterson
Printed by Johnson Printing

The paper used in this publication meets the minimum requirements of the American National Standard for Information Sciences– Permanence of Paper for Printed Library Materials, ANSI Z39.48-1992.

Table of Contents

Preface..vi
William K. Zinke

1. The Challenges and Opportunities of
   Demographic Change..1
   The Honorable David M. Walker

2. Six Key Strategies for Retaining and Recruiting
   Older Workers...13
   Susan R. Meisinger, SPHR

3. Increasing Workforce Participation Among
   Older Workers...20
   Humphrey Taylor

4. Live Longer, Work Longer: An OECD Perspective on
   Aging and Employment Policies in the United States...........39
   John P. Martin

5. Towards a Longer Worklife:
   Milestones of Finland and Finnish Institute of
   Occupational Health from 1981-2008................................59
   Juhani Ilmarinen, Ph.D.

6. The New Retirement: Myths and Models..........................72
   Helen Dennis, M.A.

7. The Role of Enabling Institutions in Tapping the
   Potential of an Aging America..83
   Scott A. Bass, Ph.D.

8. Productive Aging..94
   Robert N. Butler, M.D., Ph.D.

9. Converging Forces Require Action..................................101
   William K. Zinke

Notes and References..108

About the Authors..113

Conference Sponsors..120

Appendix 1: The Evolution of Adulthood: A New Stage,
by Dr. Elliott Jaques and William K. Zinke......................121

Appendix 2: Benefits and Opportunities Provided by
Demographic Change..131

Appendix 3: Disconnects and Dilemmas in Confronting
Demographic Change..133

Appendix 4: Reasons Why Americans 55 and Older
Continue Working After Retirement..............................136

Appendix 5: Alternatives to "Cliff Retirement"..................137

Acknowledgements

I would like to express great appreciation to all of the contributors to this book for their insightful and actionable commentaries on a topic of fundamental importance for the coming decades.

I would also like to express appreciation once again to the sponsors of the *National Conference on the New Human Resources Frontier: Utilizing Older Workers for Competitive Advantage* held in Washington, DC on June 7-8, 2007. Their support made possible a unique and stimulating event that included 20 thought leaders from the major constituencies focused on aging, retirement, and workforce planning issues.

I reserve a special debt of gratitude for Dr. Elliott Jaques, a dear friend with whom I had the pleasure of co-authoring the paper that appears in Appendix 1. Dr. Jaques presented the paper at our first conference in 2000. Unfortunately, he died in 2003 at the age of 86, and he is missed by many people around the world. His profile is included in this book.

Finally, I would like to thank my colleague Marlene Lofton for her excellent assistance in organizing all of the materials for this book.

Preface

William K. Zinke

A Personal Journey

My paternal grandfather, a New York lawyer, had a mug on his desk that he used for pencils with this saying on it: "Learn as if to live forever. Live as if to die tomorrow." My father, also a New York lawyer, kept the mug on his desk for pencils, and now it has passed to me. I consider this saying to be a core value, one that I have tried to convey to five offspring and hopefully beyond. I was a New York lawyer, too, but made a major move to Boulder, Colorado, in 1990 to enhance my quality of life after almost 40 years of working in New York City. Several years later I had the mug replicated in quantity and sent it to family, friends, clients, and acquaintances. I still retain a file with their many letters of appreciation.

In June 1969, I organized a management consulting firm named Human Resource Services, Inc. (HRS). This came one year after proposing, while Vice President-Industrial Relations at the National Association of Manufacturers (NAM), that the tired terms of Personnel/Employee Relations/Industrial Relations be changed to Human Resources as a part of stimulating companies to take a more integrated approach to human resources (HR) management. The proposal was voted down by the NAM Industrial Relations Committee. To this day I view it as one of my most successful defeats.

With a deep-seated belief that HR should be playing a center-stage role and contributing to achievement of the company's strategic objectives, rather than dealing with "administrivia" and being referred to as the "smile and file department," the focus of HRS was on strategic issues relating to HR management. Ten years after its inception, HRS organized a national survey on "Human Resources Management in U.S. Industry: Current Status and Future Directions". The results shown by the survey were groundbreaking:

- Thirty percent of companies were using HR terminology (with some even moving toward an integrated approach to HR management).

- The HR head, in many companies, moved up from the Manager or Director level to Vice President, was reporting at higher levels including the CEO.
- The HR head was expected to be more business-oriented, more proactive and strategic in focus, and was becoming a member of the top-management committee.

As a direct result of the survey, I was asked to organize the Human Resources Roundtable Group (HRRG) so that HR heads would have a twice-yearly forum to focus in a confidential setting on the strategic issues that were, or ought to be, high on their agendas. The HRRG, now in its 29th year, has moved from a national to an international to a global focus and presently has about 65 members from major companies around the world. Managing the group has required a continuous attention to the strategic issues that may be on the horizon.

All of this background explains how I connected with issues relating to the economic and social impact of demographic change. The first connection came when I read *Age Wave* by Ken Dychtwold in early 1989. Then in May of that year, I read an extensive interview in *The Wall Street Journal* with David Birch, at that time the President of Cognetics, Inc. in Cambridge, Massachusetts, and a well-known futurist. His comments stressed the impact and importance of demographic change, with an aging and shrinking workforce due to the 78 million Baby Boomers approaching retirement and sharply lower birthrates.

First National Conference in Washington, DC, June 7-8, 2000

On a lovely day in early October 1999, I sat on the lawn in Gloucester, Massachusetts, of Dr. Elliott Jaques, a renowned social scientist and author of a paper in 1965 on *Death and the Mid-Life Crisis* that has caused quite a stir over the years. His thesis was that people face a crisis at age 35, then considered to be midlife, with a psychological change occurring as they confront the reality of a life half over. The paper discussed the frequent attempts of people to remain young or at least appear youthful (e.g., buy a red convertible, remarry a younger and trophy spouse), and Dr. Jaques was thereafter known as the author of the mid-life crisis.

Elliott Jaques was also a close personal friend and someone I viewed as one of the leading thinkers of the 20th Century. During the course of a long and prolific life, he wrote more than 20 books on various aspects of work and organizational theory, and his consulting activities literally spanned the world. He died at the age of 86 in 2003, at which time he was planning a three-year consulting project with a leading company in Indonesia.

The purpose of my visit was to propose that Dr. Jaques write a paper on the later-life crisis that people face when their career job ends and they face retirement. I call this "cliff retirement" because many people face despair and depression as they confront the latter part of their lifespan without a job as an anchor and without much thought devoted to how they will spend their extended years (increased by 30 years from beginning to end of the 20th Century, with a retirement age remaining at 65 that was, established by the Social Security Act in 1935). Instead, we agreed to co-author a paper to be delivered at a conference organized by HRS in 2000, entitled "The Evolution of Adulthood: A New Stage". After discussing the first stage of early adulthood from 18 to 40, and the second stage of mid-adulthood from 40 to 62, we described a new and third stage of mature adulthood from 62 to 85 during which many people could continue to remain productively engaged (see Appendix 1 for complete text of paper).

Dr. Jaques delivered the paper at an event in Washington, DC, in June 2000, called *Meeting the Employment Needs of the 21st Century: National Conference on the Economic and Social Impact of Demographic Change*, which produced significant interest and media attention. The essential purpose of the conference was to stimulate the substantially increased utilization of workers 55 and older (workers 55+) in productive activities, paid and volunteer, for which they were ready and qualified to continue adding value. At that time, the oldest of the 78 million Baby Boomers were approaching 55, the economy was strong, the unemployment rate had been below 4.5 percent for more than one year (as low as 4.1% for the period of October-December 1999), and there was a major focus on "the war for talent." HRS published a book in January 2001 based on edited texts of presentations made at the conference and contributed material, entitled *Working Through Demographic Change: How Older Americans Can Sustain the Nation's Prosperity*. This was followed by the burst of the dot-com bubble in March and the subsequent years required for recovery from a recession.

Second National Conference in Washington, DC, June 7-8, 2007

While continuing to advocate the utilization of workers 55+ in various ways and waiting for the economy to improve, I began to plot a future course of action that resulted in organizing a follow-on event in June 2007. With a strong economy and the oldest of the Baby Boomers reaching the early retirement age of 62 in 2008 and each year thereafter through 2025 at the rate of 4.28 million per year, the second conference was planned as the launching platform for the Center for Productive Longevity (CPL), a 501(c)(3) non-profit created and funded by HRS. The purpose of this event, *National Conference on the New Human Resources Frontier: Utilizing Older Workers for Competitive Advantage*, and the stated mission of CPL were the same as for the first conference.

As I write this preface, the U.S. is in another economic downturn that many predict will develop into a recession. However, it is now clear that the U.S. civilian workforce is aging and shrinking, with talent shortages in the range of four-ten million people projected by 2010. Workers 55+ are the fastest-growing sector of all age groups in the civilian workforce, with an annual growth rate from 2006 to 2016 projected by the U.S. Bureau of Labor Statistics (BLS) at more than five times that of the overall workforce. And recent survey data indicates that almost 80 percent of the Baby Boomers intend to continue in productive activities after retirement, a majority on a part-time basis.

What we have in America is the convergence of two forces: employers seeking talent to maintain their productivity and profitability on one side, and a substantial majority of the Baby Boomers ready and qualified to continue working beyond traditional retirement age on the other. These Baby Boomers constitute a large and growing talent pool of people with experience, expertise, seasoned judgment, and proven performance. They want to continue working for a variety of reasons: the need for additional income to maintain a standard of living, particularly with the ongoing subprime mortgage fiasco that has spread to the entire economy; the housing crisis, which has reduced the value of homes for many people throughout the country; a credit crunch and increased interest rates that have further constrained economic growth; the need to maintain healthcare coverage; and a variety of other reasons including the desire to continue adding value and to remain socially connected.

There are several hurdles that need to be overcome:

- There is an entrenched mindset in America and other industrialized countries that when people reach a certain age, regardless of their ability to continue adding value, they are "over the hill" and "out of the game." Since I am over 80 and lead an extremely active life, I happily tell people that I am over the hill and have learned that you pick up speed going down the other side. Ageism, however, continues to flourish in this country. What is needed is a national campaign to change the pervasive mindset about aging and retirement.

- A second challenge is that employers (private, public, and non-profit) must develop flexible workplace policies, practices, and compensation packages that will be attractive to workers 55+, many of whom want to work part-time versus full-time. Less than 20 percent of companies have done so to date.

- A third is that there are many governmental laws and policies that discourage employers from utilizing older workers and that create a disincentive for older workers to continue in employment; these laws and policies must be changed to provide incentives rather than disincentives.

These and other hurdles will be addressed in this book, which is intended to reach a wide range of constituencies on the national and international levels because all of the developed countries are confronted with the same challenges relating to demographic change. The constituencies include employers in all sectors, particularly people responsible for HR management and workforce planning; leadership in organizations that are concerned about talent management and succession planning; people 55+ or approaching that stage who need or want to continue working; government officials who need to take action on legal and policy change, particularly those with responsibility for social programs that are financially unsustainable; economists and futurists who are concerned about the continued growth of the national and global economies; and all other people who are or ought to be concerned about the economic and social impact of demographic change.

This book is published by CPL not simply to provide information, but rather to stimulate action: the substantially increased utilization of workers 55+ who are ready and qualified to continue in productive activities, paid and volunteer. Failure to use this large and growing talent pool can slow the country's economic growth and development; intensify the unsustainability of Social Security, Medicare, and other social programs; create serious talent shortages in many business sectors; and increase healthcare costs because research demonstrates that older Americans who don't remain productively engaged and socially connected have more health problems than those who do. It will also reduce the standard of living for many Americans who have saved too little for their extended longevity, seen their home values diminish because of the subprime mortgage fiasco, and are dealing with significantly higher prices for gasoline and food while their investments have lost value in an economic downturn.

These negative forces are not limited to the U.S. but relate to all of the industrialized countries, some of which have older populations and lower birthrates. We can wait to deal with the frequently-stated problems and potential crises, or we can seize the benefits and opportunities of demographic change (see Appendix 2). The purpose of CPL in publishing this book is to stimulate the latter result.

It has been said: "A window of opportunity won't open itself." Our hope is that this book will help to open that window.

The Challenges and Opportunities of Demographic Change

The Honorable David M. Walker

President and Chief Executive Officer, Peter G. Peterson Foundation and former Comptroller General, U.S. Government Accountability Office

During the past 50 years, the United States has been the beneficiary of favorable demographic trends, such as the entry of women into the workforce, which ensured a growing labor force and an expanding economy. This will soon change, however, as the 78 million baby boomers begin to retire. Entitlement programs, such as Social Security and Medicare, will begin to feel the strain as more and more Americans retire and collect benefits or require services. At the same time, lower birth rates mean fewer new workers will be available to replace those individuals who have left the labor force. The challenge before us is how best to care for our aging population while exploring ways to sustain the size and quality of our labor force, including providing opportunities for America's seniors to continue to work if they so choose.

Demographic Realities

In the future, Americans 65 and older will comprise a larger share of the U.S. population. This population segment is projected to increase from 12.4 percent in 2000 to 19.6 percent in 2030 and continue to grow through 2050. This is due, in part, to increases in life expectancy. On average, by 2020 men who reach age 65 are expected to live another 17 years–up from just 13 years in 1970. Women have experienced a similar rise in longevity.

These increases in life expectancy have not, however, resulted in older Americans working longer. In fact, some individuals are now spending as much as one third of their lives in full retirement.

The challenge associated with a growing elderly population is complicated by the fact that lower fertility rates, along with a leveling off of women's participation in the labor force, is slowing workforce growth. Although women's share of the labor force increased dramatically between 1950 and 2000–from 30 percent to 47 percent–their share of the labor force is projected to remain at around 48 percent over the next 50 years. By 2025, total labor force growth is expected to be less than a fifth of what it is today.

The aging of the baby boom generation, longer life expectancy, and fertility rates near the replacement level are expected to significantly increase the elderly dependency ratio–the estimated number of people age 15 to 64 relative to those age 65 and over. In 1960, there were more than five people age 15 to 64 for every person age 65 and older. That ratio decreased to 3.4 to one in 2000 and is projected to eventually drop to around two to one. The result is that fewer younger workers are paying into programs such as Social Security and Medicare.

The aging of the population also has implications for the nation's economy. If labor force growth continues to slow as projected, fewer workers will be available to produce goods and services. Without a major increase in productivity or higher-than-projected immigration rates, low labor force growth will slow economic growth and, by extension, government revenues. The timing could not be worse. Traditional sources of government funding will become constrained just as claims under federal retirement and health care programs begin to soar.

Retirement Security

Our growing fiscal imbalance will affect many aspects of American society. Key among them is retirement planning. In the United States, a secure retirement has traditionally included several elements: Social Security, Medicare or Medicaid, private pensions and health benefits, and personal savings. Some of these elements may not be as reliable or generous in the future as they were in the past. For example, federal spending on Social Security, Medicare, and Medicaid represent about eight percent of the gross domestic product (GDP) today. If unchanged, by 2055 entitlement spending could rise to 20 percent of GDP. That means that one in five dollars out of the entire economy would go to these three federal programs, a level that threatens the future growth and competitiveness of the U.S. economy.

As a result, Americans can no longer take for granted that federal entitlement programs will continue in their present form. The combination of increasing life expectancy and declining birth rates will put huge strains on both public and private retirement benefit systems. For example, in 1960 more than five workers were paying into Social Security for every retiree drawing benefits. By 2040, that ratio will have dwindled to about two to one. Soon afterward, the reserves in the Social Security "trust funds" are expected to be exhausted. At that point, there will only be enough revenue from payroll taxes to pay about 75 cents of every dollar of promised benefits.[1]

Medicare's future funding needs are even more troubling. Medicare's shortfall is roughly seven times greater than Social Security, and the Medicare trust fund for hospital payments will be exhausted in 2019. As a result, the changes to this program will be needed sooner and could be much more dramatic over time. Younger baby boomers have good reason to be concerned about their promised entitlement benefits, although the ones who should really be worried are their children and grandchildren.

Problems with retirement security, however, are not limited to public sector programs. In recent years, we have seen cutbacks in employer-sponsored pension plans and health benefits. The days of generous "cradle-to-grave" benefit packages are largely gone. These days, even life-long employment at a Fortune 500 company is no guarantee of health insurance in retirement. In addition, although the percentage of workers being covered by an employer pension plan is around 50 percent—about the same as 1980 levels—the type of retirement income benefits being offered has changed dramatically. Defined benefit pension plans were standard for many decades at U.S. companies. Under this type of pension plan, employers provided a retiree with a stated monthly income for life. In recent years, however, a number of major corporations have announced pension freezes, which means that employee pension benefits stop accruing as of a certain date.

Further, the government agency responsible for insuring all or part of these defined benefit plans, the Pension Benefit Guaranty Corporation (PBGC), is also at risk. In 2003, GAO designated PBGC's single-employer insurance program as "high-risk," a designation that remains today. The PBGC went from a $9.7 billion surplus in 2000 to a $23 billion deficit in 2005. The situation has improved somewhat over the last two years, as the deficit is now $14.1 billion. Further recent legislation, among other things, should help raise certain premium revenues for PBGC. Despite these somewhat encouraging signs, PBGC remains exposed to possibly significant claims, especially from financially weak sponsors in troubled industries. For example, in 2007 PBGC estimates $66 billion in underfunding exposure to those plan sponsors, classified as "reasonably possible," whose credit ratings are below investment grade or meet one or more financial distress criteria.

The baby boomers, especially younger boomers, will be the first generation with significant account balances in defined contribution plans, which include 401(k) plans. Employers generally match all or part of worker contributions up to stated limits. As a result, it is increasingly up to the worker to plan, save, and invest for his or her retirement. Defined contribution plans do have many positive features. In a world in which the average worker will change jobs several times during a career, portability of benefits is a huge advantage. Unlike many defined benefit plans, 401(k) plans can follow a worker from job to job. Growing evidence, however, shows that many workers are failing to take full advantage of these plans. A recent GAO report on defined contribution plans estimated that 33 percent of workers who were offered such a plan by their current employer were not participating.[2] In addition, although defined benefit pensions are untouchable until retirement, today employees are able to dip into or even spend their entire 401(k) balances before retirement–and too many do. This failure to retain savings until retirement is a growing concern. Combined, these trends suggest a potential lower standard of living for many retirees and a growing financial burden for future generations.

Given these trends, America's low saving rate is particularly alarming. Many baby boomers are falling short in accumulating the large sums needed to provide a comfortable old age. Some, undoubtedly, are counting on Social Security to carry them through retirement. Yet from the start, Social Security was intended to be supplemented by private pensions, personal savings, and other income. This means that all of us are going to have to take greater responsibility for our own financial futures. Americans will need to plan better, save more, invest more wisely, and preserve more of their savings if they want a financially secure retirement.

Working Longer

Beginning in 2008, the oldest of the baby boomers are eligible to leave the workforce in large numbers as they reach 62. Data show that the boomers are living longer than previous generations, yet many expect to retire just as early as or earlier than their parents. Longer retirements also underscore the importance of policies that encourage future workforce growth and longer working lives in our knowledge-based economy. Many baby boomers may need to defer retirement and work longer, even if only part-time, to maintain their standard of living into their 60s, 70s, and beyond. The hope is that more Americans will work longer or at least transition from full-time jobs to part-time work before retiring outright.

Between the retirement of the baby boomers and slower workforce growth, some industries are already facing skill shortages. Too little is being done, however, to encourage older workers, with their valuable training and experience, to stay on the job–a key finding in a recent GAO report.[3] In fact, older workers are one of America's most underutilized assets.

In December 2006, GAO convened a forum on engaging and retaining older workers. Participants included a diverse array of experts, including employers from AARP's "Best Employers for Workers over 50" program, and representatives from business groups, unions, academia, and federal agencies. The forum addressed how employers, employees, and the federal government can help older Americans work longer and better prepare for retirement. The discussion focused on key obstacles faced by workers who want to work longer, as well as those faced by employers who need to retain and recruit workers who are near or past traditional retirement age.

Some of the obstacles that hinder continued work at older ages include employer perceptions about the cost of employing older workers; employee perceptions about the costs and benefits of continued work; and changes in industry and job skill requirements, which may hinder older workers from remaining employed or finding suitable new employment.

Many employers cite compensation, especially the rising cost of health insurance, and training costs as key barriers to hiring and retaining older workers. In addition, forum participants reported that many employers undervalue their experienced workers, instead gearing their succession planning toward younger people. Some forum participants cited negative stereotypes surrounding older workers, such as the perception that they are less productive and produce lower-quality work than their younger counterparts. Many employers also believe that older workers are resistant to change. Finally, but not least, it was suggested that some employers are hesitant to hire older workers for fear of age discrimination lawsuits. Although many businesses claim to be interested in recruiting older workers, GAO studies have found that few employers have developed programs to accomplish this.

In addition to employer resistance to utilizing older workers, they face strong economic and other incentives to retire. Forum participants noted that a "culture of retirement" exists in this country that encourages workers to claim retirement benefits and stop working as early as possible. The availability of Social Security at age 62 and high effective tax rates on earnings between age 62 and Social Security's full retirement age can discourage individuals from continuing to work once they start claiming benefits. Those who receive Social Security benefits but have not yet reached the full retirement age have their benefits reduced by one dollar for every two or three dollars that they earn above a set threshold due to the Social Security earnings test. Not surprisingly, workers who claim Social Security benefits at 62 may conclude it is not worthwhile to continue working.

Furthermore, the structure of traditional defined benefit pension plans may promote retirement because pension laws have limited working for the same employer while receiving benefits. Although the Pension Protection Act of 2006 does allow individuals age 62 and older who are still working to receive some benefits, it is too soon to determine what the impact of this policy change will be. In addition to these financial incentives, jobs that are physically demanding or have inflexible schedules that compete with family care-giving needs also provide strong disincentives to continued work.

For some, the choice to retire is driven by a lack of suitable job opportunities. Some employers are reluctant to offer flexible work arrangements, such as part-time work. In addition, globalization also seems to be having a disproportionate impact on older workers. Forum participants reported that downsizing industries, such as manufacturing, tend to have a disproportionate number of older workers in their labor force. Many low-skill jobs held by older workers have been automated, eliminated, or outsourced. At the same time, displaced older workers may lack the necessary training to make a career change.

GAO reports have found that older workers who lose their job are less likely than younger workers to find other employment.

Some forum participants shared examples of best practices and lessons learned from their efforts to engage and retain older workers. These included using non-traditional recruiting techniques to identify and recruit older workers; employing flexible work situations and adapting job designs to meet the preferences and physical constraints of older workers; offering the right mix of benefits and incentives to attract older workers; treating all employees in a fair and consistent manner and employing a consistent performance management system to prevent age discrimination complaints; and providing employees with financial literacy skills to ensure they have a realistic plan to provide for retirement security.

The forum also discussed possible strategies for employing older workers. These included conducting a national campaign to help change the national mindset about work at older ages; holding a national discussion about what "old" means to help change the culture of retirement; strengthening financial literacy education to help workers prepare to retire; creating a clearinghouse of best recruiting, hiring, and retention practices for older workers; making the federal government a model employer for the nation in how it recruits and retains older workers; creating a key federal role in partnerships to implement these strategies; and considering specific legislation or regulations to increase flexibility for employers and employees to create new employment models.

A Way Forward

GAO has issued a report entitled "21st Century Challenges: Reexamining the Base of the Federal Government"[4] that seeks to stimulate debate about many long-standing government programs and policies, including those designed to ensure a secure retirement for the American people. Drawing on GAO's institutional knowledge and extensive program evaluation and performance assessment work for Congress, this report includes more than 200 questions reflecting the types of hard choices that policymakers face in transforming government missions and operations. Social Security, Medicare, health care, private pensions, and personal savings are among the many topics covered. Some of the questions posed include:

- How should Social Security be reformed to provide for long-term program solvency and sustainability while also ensuring adequate benefits? For example, should policymakers increase the retirement age, restructure benefits, increase taxes, and/or create individual accounts?

- How can we make our current Medicare and Medicaid programs sustainable? For example, should the eligibility requirements for these programs, such as age or income, be modified?

- How can we perform a systematic reexamination of our current health care system? For example, could public and private entities work jointly to establish formal reexamination processes that would (1) define and update, as needed, a minimum core of essential health care services, (2) ensure that all Americans have access to the defined minimum core services, (3) allocate responsibility for financing these services among such entities as government, employers, and individuals, and (4) provide the opportunity for individuals to obtain additional services at their discretion and cost?

- What changes should be made to enhance the retirement income security of workers while protecting the fiscal integrity of the PBGC insurance program? Options here include increasing transparency in underfunded plans, modifying PBGC's premium structure and insurance guarantees, reforming plan funding rules, or restricting benefit increases and the distribution of lump sum benefits in some underfunded plans.

- How can existing policies be reformed to encourage income preservation strategies so that retirement income lasts an individual's entire life? One possibility might be benefit annuitization.

- How can existing policies and programs be reformed to encourage older workers to work longer and to facilitate phased retirement approaches to employment? For example, should older workers have the option of receiving a partial pension while they continue to work?

- Should the existing tax system be changed from an income to a consumption base? Would such a change help respond to challenges posed by demographic, economic, and technological changes? How would such a change affect savings and work incentives?

In addition to broad-based questions like these, GAO has developed criteria for evaluating Social Security reform proposals, set broad goals for reforming the defined benefit system, and identified options that need to be considered in connection with health care reform.

If Social Security reform is adopted in the very near future, it will likely involve few, if any, changes for individuals beyond or near retirement age. Most changes for younger workers will likely be phased in over time. Possible changes that have been proposed in the past include higher normal retirement ages, lower income replacement rates for middle- and upper-income individuals, a strengthened minimum benefit for low-income individuals, a modified cost-of-living index, and possibly a higher taxable wage base. All proposals should be evaluated as packages that strike a balance among individual reform elements and important interactive effects. Comprehensive proposals can be evaluated against three basic criteria:

- the extent to which a proposal achieves sustainable solvency and how it would affect the economy and the federal budget; the relative balance struck between the goals of individual equity and income adequacy; and

- the ease with which a given proposal could be implemented, administered, and explained to the public.

In addition to a reformed defined benefit Social Security program, serious consideration should be given to a supplemental and mandatory individual saving program. These accounts could be funded by an additional modest payroll tax withholding with the money being deposited in a real trust fund. Individuals would have various pooled investment options, much like the Thrift Savings Plan that is available to federal workers.

The stability and sustainability of the nation's pension system are also vitally important. The Pension Protection Act of 2006 (PPA) is the most comprehensive reform of the nation's pension laws since the enactment of the Employee Retirement Income Security Act of 1974 (ERISA, P.L. 93-406). It establishes new funding requirements for defined benefit pensions and includes reforms that will affect cash balance pension plans, defined contribution plans, and deferred compensation plans for executives and highly compensated employees. The Act also requires employers to disclose more information about pension funding; restricts benefit payments and accruals in underfunded plans; and clarifies, prospectively, that cash balance pension plans do not violate legal prohibitions on age discrimination in employee benefits.

Despite these reforms, challenges remain. The PPA's overall impact on the PBGC's single-employer program's deficit is unclear. The PPA will not fully close potential plan funding gaps, and it provides funding relief to plan sponsors in troubled industries. As a result, PBGC may be exposed to additional terminations of large underfunded plans. PPA is also unlikely to reverse the long-term decline of the DB system or help PBGC make up its current deficit, as stricter funding requirements and higher premiums may lead sponsors to terminate or freeze their plans.

As discussed earlier, many Americans may need to work longer, full-time or part-time, to maintain their standard of living in retirement. In this regard, the PPA would allow, beginning in 2007, a defined benefit plan to make in-service distributions to a participant who has reached age 62 and continues to work for the same employer.

In reforming our health care system and Medicare, the public requires better understanding of the differences between wants and needs. The public also requires more information about benefit affordability and sustainability at both the individual and aggregate level. To provide an acceptable level of healthcare to the baby boomers, healthcare providers, consumers, and especially policymakers will need to fundamentally rethink how health care in this country is defined, delivered, and financed. That is true for both the public and private sectors. Unlimited individual wants will need to be weighed against broader societal needs, and decisions will need to be made about how responsibility for financing health care should be divided among employers, individuals, and government. Individuals wanting more than a basic level of coverage might need to set aside resources to pay for it. Clearly, such a dramatic change would require an appropriate transition period. Ideally, health care reform proposals will:

- align incentives for providers and consumers to make prudent choices about health insurance coverage and prudent decisions about the use of medical services;

- foster transparency with respect to the value and costs of care; and

- ensure accountability from health plans and providers to meet standards for appropriate use and quality.

Selected potential health care reform approaches the nation should consider include:

- Leveraging technology and pursuing more managed care and income-related premium options.

- Leveraging the government's purchasing authority to foster value-based purchasing for health care products and services.

- Developing a set of national practice standards to help reduce cost, improve outcomes, and reduce litigation.

- Revising certain federal tax preferences for health care to encourage the efficient use of appropriate care.

- Limiting spending growth for government-sponsored health care programs to a percentage of the federal budget or the GDP.

- Developing a core set of basic and essential services with supplemental coverage being available as an option but at a cost. The Federal Employees Health Benefits Program could serve as a model.

- Incorporating more incentives and accountability mechanisms to encourage individuals to assume more personal responsibility for their health and wellness.

In the final analysis, health care reform should achieve the following four key objectives: universal access to basic and essential health care coverage, a health care budget for the federal government, a national and evidence-based set of practice standards, and incentives and accountability for each individual's physical health and wellness. Additionally, the federal government should seek to lead by example in reforming its own healthcare programs.

Conclusion

The United States is at a critical crossroads. Americans can no longer take for granted that the Social Security, Medicare, and Medicaid programs will continue in their present form. Every working-age citizen is going to have to take more responsibility for his or her own financial future. The aging of the baby boom generation presents both a challenge and an opportunity for our nation. The number of older workers is a large and growing part of the total population. They represent a substantially underutilized national resource with the potential to improve the economic well-being for themselves and the nation. Engaging and retaining older workers are critical for promoting economic growth, improving federal finances, and shoring up retirees' income security.

Given the right mix of incentives, programs, and job designs, we have an opportunity today to engage those who wish to work later in life, thereby reinventing the traditional concept of retirement, helping to bolster individuals' retirement security, and fostering economic growth. With the oldest members of the baby boom generation becoming eligible to begin collecting early Social Security benefits in 2008, time is running out to seize this opportunity.

Six Key HR Strategies for Retaining and Recruiting Older Workers

Susan R. Meisinger, SPHR

President and Chief Executive Officer, Society for Human Resource Management, world's largest association devoted to HR management with over 225,000 members

The business case for retaining and fully engaging older workers is now widely accepted. And yet, many employers are ill-prepared to accommodate older workers' needs. According to a 2007 Manpower Inc. study, only 21 percent of employers surveyed around the world have mapped out strategies for keeping older employees, and the Center for Retirement Research at Boston College found employers "lukewarm" to the idea.

By contrast, employers in Japan and Singapore are in the forefront with plans to retain older workers, with 83 percent and 53 percent of those countries, respectively, having retention strategies. This is, in part, attributable to laws and incentive programs in those countries that promote retaining and recruiting older workers. Among 1,000 U.S. employers surveyed by Manpower Inc., only 28 percent have a formal retention strategy for older workers, and only 18 percent have a recruitment strategy.

What's needed at this critical juncture is a commitment to action by C-Suite executives, including Chief Human Resource Officers and other senior HR executives and their teams. With this in mind, I want to outline a set of six key strategies HR professionals need to put into place to help their organizations compete by retaining and leveraging their employees aged 50 and older.

Background on Society for Human Resource Management (SHRM)

By way of background, I should note that the issue of engaging and retaining older workers has been a top priority at SHRM for several years. Consequently, we have been active on several fronts in raising awareness and promoting strategies among HR professionals and in the business, academic, and governmental communities.

In 2006, for instance, we joined with AARP and more than 20 other organizations to form the Aging Workforce Advisory Council, which is raising awareness about the role of older workers and supporting initiatives to retain and engage them. I am honored to serve as Vice Chair of this Council. We have also participated in the White House Conference on Aging and the December 2006 GAO Comptroller General's Forum on Engaging and Retaining Older Workers. Currently, we are taking part in the Phased Retirement Working Group of the Workplace Flexibility 2010 initiative, organized by the Georgetown University Law Center and the Alfred P. Sloan Foundation.

We have also conducted and disseminated considerable research on workforce trends—some of which I cite below—which provides insights into issues such as the impact of Baby Boomer retirements and potential talent and skills shortages. In addition, our Government Affairs team and our chapters and state councils actively advocate on issues related to older workers with legislative and governmental bodies at the local, state, and federal levels.

The Challenge

The popular film, *A Perfect Storm*, depicts the plight of a New England fishing boat caught in the confluence of two powerful weather fronts and a hurricane. Well, a perfect storm is brewing for the U.S. economy. Our workforce is aging and shrinking, Baby Boomers are getting ready to retire, new entrants into the workforce lack the skills employers are seeking, and companies are exporting both high and low skill jobs to countries where labor is relatively cheap and increasingly well educated.

The storm clouds are looking ominous this year as the first wave of the nation's 78 million Baby Boomers reaches 62—the Social Security early retirement age. There are also serious concerns at the other end of the spectrum. In late 2006, SHRM teamed with the Conference Board, Corporate Voices for Working Families, and the Partnership for 21st Century Skills on a significant report, entitled "Are They Really Ready to Work?"

That report, based on responses from 431 HR professionals and interviews with over 400 employers, looked at the skills employers say are important to be successful in the workplace, and whether new entrants—including high school, junior college, and college graduates—have these skills. Let me quote the report's stark conclusion: "The future workforce is here, and it is ill-prepared."

The good news is that most Baby Boomers will not retire in the traditional sense of the word. According to AARP research, 69 percent of U.S. employees aged 45-74 plan to work in some form during "retirement." Of course, many older workers feel they cannot afford to retire because they have not saved enough or because they would lose their valuable health care coverage if they left their employment.

On the other hand, many are healthy, love their work, and want to continue being actively engaged in their careers. The bottom line is that retaining these older workers should be a goal for every organization. Despite the "perfect storm" that I and others have described, opportunities still abound for those who are willing to seize the moment.

Six Strategies

HR professionals are in a unique position to ensure that older workers have the incentives to continue contributing to their organizations well beyond what has been considered the normal retirement age. To achieve this goal, they need to employ at least some of the following six strategies in a coordinated, systematic fashion.

These six strategies will only be successful if they are implemented within a work environment that recognizes the importance of generational diversity. This means that ongoing diversity training is essential to maintain a productive and harmonious workplace environment that promotes retention among each age group, including those aged 50+.

1. Strategic Workforce Planning

The first and most basic of the six strategies is strategic workforce planning. Simply stated, organizations need to analyze their near and longer-term business plans to better understand their critical talent needs over the next five to ten years. The process requires periodic interviews with senior- and mid-level managers to predict the timing of retirements and other changes in the most crucial workforce segments.

Having this projection allows HR teams to implement targeted recruitment and talent management tactics to keep their organizations functioning smoothly as employees retire or exit for other reasons. Developing succession plans and replacement charts is also an essential component of a solid plan to keep operations running optimally.

Given that aging employees and shortages of skilled workers are becoming major concerns, one would assume that most organizations have begun planning for these contingencies. Unfortunately, 36 percent of the respondents in a March 2007 SHRM online survey said their organizations were just becoming aware of issues related to the coming retirement surge. Another 45 percent said they were beginning to examine strategies to address these issues, and only 8 percent said their organizations had implemented programs to deal with the loss of their talented older workers.

2. Knowledge Transfer

A second strategy is to preserve the knowledge of older workers through knowledge transfer programs. Losing the institutional memory of these workers can be a major blow to any organization. Here again, the numbers are disappointing: The 2005 SHRM Future Labor Pool survey showed that only 28 percent of the companies surveyed have knowledge transfer programs in place, and nearly three out of ten organizations said they have no plans to develop them.

These programs can take various shapes. Some years ago, Raytheon Vision Systems, knowing that more than 35 percent of its workforce could retire by 2009, created a training program called "Leave-A-Legacy." This program pairs employees nearing retirement with high-potential subordinate employees in mentoring relationships. Since not every near-retiree has great teaching skills, the company also uses third-party coaches who facilitate the transfer of knowledge. Other organizations videotape retiring workers talking about key aspects of their jobs, while still others establish e-mail pipelines to retirees who agree to answer current workers' questions.

3. Flexible Work Programs

A third key strategy is providing flexible work programs that allow employees to ease into retirement gradually. This can be a win-win situation for employees and employers. These programs include flexible work schedules, telecommuting options, and bridge jobs that could be part-time, full-time, or consulting on a project-by-project basis. In SHRM's 2005 Future Labor Pool Survey, 40 percent of the respondents indicated their organizations had flexible scheduling, and 25 percent had bridge employment opportunities.

Home Depot has been particularly effective with flexible work options for its older employees. For example, Home Depot's "snowbird" program allows some older employees to work in its stores near their winter homes in southern states from October to May and in northern states near their summer homes during the summer and fall.

4. Phased Retirement

Phased retirement–which lets employees receive partial pensions and work reduced hours–is a fourth strategy. Phased retirement policies had been restricted until 2007 because employers were not allowed by law to pay retirement benefits from a defined benefits pension plan until an employee had terminated employment or had reached the plan's normal retirement age. However, the new Pension Protection Act has lifted that restriction beginning January 1, 2007.

In May 2007, the Internal Revenue Service issued final regulations on the normal retirement age for a phased retirement program. SHRM had provided comments and suggestions to the IRS on the proposed regulations, and, among others, the IRS accepted SHRM's recommendation to delete the 59 age requirement for phased retirement participants. The regulation-writing process is not over, and SHRM will continue to track developments and provide comments when appropriate.

The Pension Protection Act clearly helps to make phased retirement a more viable option for many employers. Consequently, we expect the number of companies providing this option to increase. In SHRM's 2003 Older Worker Survey, only about ten percent of the organizations polled had phased retirement programs. It will be interesting to see how this percentage changes during the next couple of years.

5. Targeted Benefits and Training Programs

A fifth key strategy is to provide benefits and training opportunities that are targeted for older workers. Since these benefits can be a powerful incentive for retention and recruitment, HR teams should conduct opinion surveys among their older workers to determine which career options and specific benefits would be most valued. According to a 2005 Towers Perrin survey of 1,500 workers 50+ employed by large U.S. companies, health care coverage and competitive retirement benefits are at the top of the desired benefits list.

To attract and retain older workers, many companies are now offering medical coverage for part-time workers, the option to buy long-term care coverage, and elder care and related programs. Elder care is a particular concern for Baby Boomers ages 45 to 65, who are often "sandwiched" between the need to care for their children and for their aging parents. Wellness programs, including fitness resources, are increasingly popular.

Older workers also value training and development opportunities that help them to grow, tackle new challenges, and explore new directions. Among other innovative approaches, IBM has launched a $2 million program that will pay for tuition, licensing, and interim salaries for older employees who want to transition to new careers as math and science teachers.

6. Innovative Recruitment Programs

Finally, devising innovative recruitment programs that target workers aged 50+ represents a sixth key strategy. I will again briefly highlight Home Depot as a model in targeted recruiting. The "snowbird" program I mentioned earlier is part of Home Depot's "Passion Never Retires" recruitment effort, aimed at older workers.

In 2004, Home Depot partnered with AARP to promote job opportunities among AARP's 35 million members. Several other major companies saw the wisdom in that approach, and in 2005 AARP launched its National Employer Team initiative with 13 partners. Today, there are 30 companies in The National Employer Team, and its website includes links to all of the partner companies, with information about their benefits programs, locations, and work conditions, as well as job vacancies and application forms.

An equally innovative approach was followed by Proctor & Gamble and Eli Lilly, which teamed up in 2003 to found "YourEncore." This unique service recruits and markets highly skilled retirees–especially scientists, engineers, and product developers– for short-term assignments at member companies. Non-member companies are also able to access the retiree experts, but at higher engagement fees. The retirees are employed by "YourEncore," which provides all necessary administrative, marketing, and accounting support.

Many companies are using creative recruitment tactics to re–employ their own retirees. Monsanto, for instance, offers part-time re–employment opportunities with no loss of retirement benefits to workers who have been retired from the company at least six months. John Deere, which currently has 25,000 retirees, employs an executive with direct responsibility for retiree relations. This individual keeps retirees connected through regular communications and invitations to company events. John Deere offers its retirees temporary work assignments, consulting and contract work, telecommuting, and part- and full-time work programs.

Moving Forward

SHRM will continue to help HR professionals take the lead in promoting the six strategies I have outlined above. At the same time, there are more lessons to be learned, and we commend the Center for Productive Longevity for helping to raise awareness among employers and employees. SHRM is proud to have been a presenter at and a sponsor for the Center's June 7-8, 2007 *National Conference on the New HR Frontier: Utilizing Older Workers for Competitive Advantage.*

The title of that conference accurately describes our mission. HR professionals are at a crossroads. We are facing a new HR challenge, and we must be even more passionate and creative in finding ways to fully utilize older workers for competitive advantage. It's been said that the best way to predict the future is to make it. We can make a huge difference for the future of our own organizations and, in so doing, for the well-being of our country.

Increasing Workforce Participation Among Older Workers

Humphrey Taylor

Chairman, Harris Poll, a service of Harris Interactive, previously President and Chief Executive Officer, Harris

The research reported in this chapter has been influenced by the assumption that increases in longevity, and the aging of the Baby Boomers, will lead to a continuing decline in the ratio of workers to older people who are not working unless a substantially larger proportion of older people stay in the work force. A second assumption is that it will be difficult and expensive for employers to recruit and retain enough workers unless more older people are employed who are qualified to continue in productive activities. These trends would, many economists believe, have a very serious impact on the economy and on our standards of living. The key questions addressed by the research reviewed here are: What might be done by employers and others to increase the numbers of older workers who are qualified to continue adding value? And what could they do to attract, motivate, and retain these workers?

Most of this chapter is based on survey research conducted over the last few years. However, it also draws on earlier research conducted over the last 30 years.

Summary of Previous Research

For more than 30 years Harris Interactive and its predecessor, Louis Harris and Associates, conducted many important surveys about older workers. These have examined the hopes, fears, and expectations of workers as they look to their later lives and the experiences of older workers and retirees. They have also examined the attitudes and behaviors of employers as they view older workers, and what they can do to attract, retain, and motivate older workers with experience, expertise, and proven performance.

Some of the findings of this body of research were:

- Most people in many countries have been strongly opposed to employers having a mandatory retirement age. A 1974 Harris survey in the United States reported a national consensus among people of all ages who were opposed to mandatory retirement. This led to the 1978 law that made it illegal for most employees, with some exceptions.

- Older people were generally healthier, happier and more active than many people (including even older people) believed. There was a tendency to underestimate the abilities and skills that older workers bring to their work.

- Retirement was viewed by many as a time to be active rather than a time for passivity, rest, and relaxation. Many retirees wanted to engage in new activities both at work and beyond.

- Large numbers of people over 60 believed they were living through the best years of their lives. And many more said their lives had never been better.

- Most people defined old age in terms of physical and mental ability rather than in chronological age.

- Between 1974 and 1999, the number of older people worried about such things as crime, money, health, and loneliness declined substantially. Younger people, however, were more likely than older people to see these as major concerns for the elderly.

- Retirement is no longer the same thing as stopping work. Most workers expected to do some work–full time, part-time or moving in and out of work–after they retired from full-time employment in their career jobs.

- Employers, while somewhat aware of future shortages of skilled labor and the need to make better use of the talents and experience of older workers, were not doing much to attract, retain, or motivate older workers.

- Many corporate employers believed that older workers with managerial, technical, or professional skills were potentially valuable to their companies.

- Although many employers had positive experiences with their older workers, retaining them had been very low on their list of priorities.

The rest of this chapter draws on a series of major research projects conducted by Harris Interactive with AgeWave for Merrill Lynch and HSBC in 2006 and 2007. In most cases the survey data speaks for itself.

1. Working After Retirement

Retirement used to mean stopping work. Not any more. The great majority (74%) of Baby Boomers reported in 2006 that they expected to work after retirement. Only 19 percent said they did not expect to work again for pay after they retire.

If retirement does not mean stopping work, what does it mean? For the great majority of Baby Boomers it means doing something different—working in a different line of work, going back and forth between periods of work and leisure, working part-time, or starting their own business.

Further evidence that retirement for most people does not mean the end of work is that, on average, adults intend to retire at 61 but do not expect to stop working completely until they are 70. In other words, on average they expect to work for nine years after they retire. This pattern of working after retirement is not completely new, nor is it just a hope or a wish. A substantial proportion of people aged 60-70 in 2006 described themselves as "retired and working" (29%) or as "not retired" (19%). Furthermore, another 23 percent said they were retired and not working but would work for pay again if a suitable job were available.

Some commentators have argued that older people work only because they need the money. Others have suggested that it is not about the money but reflects a desire to stay active and connected and to provide a sense of self worth. Our data show that all of these reasons for working are very common. Furthermore, many Baby Boomers (45%) plan to work later in life in order to obtain health insurance. Clearly it is not "just about the money," but the money is very important.

Exhibit 1

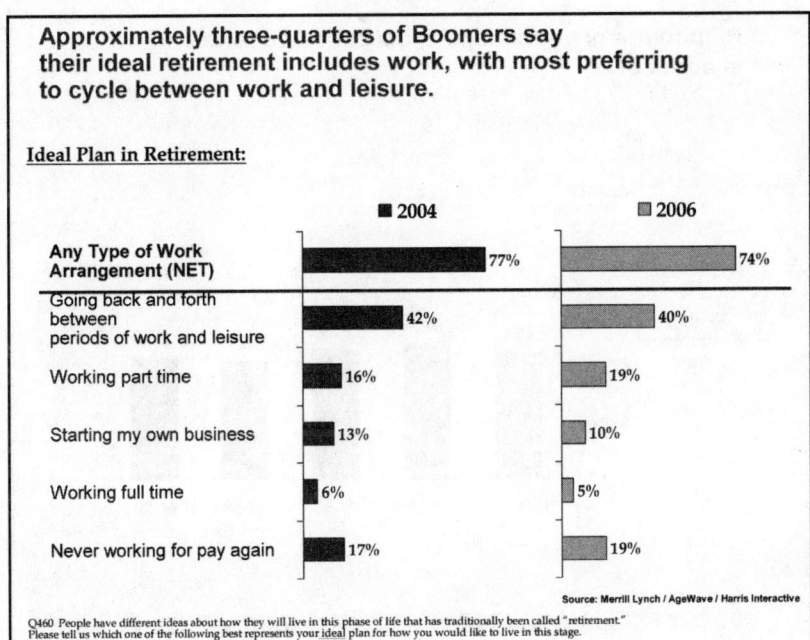

Exhibit 2

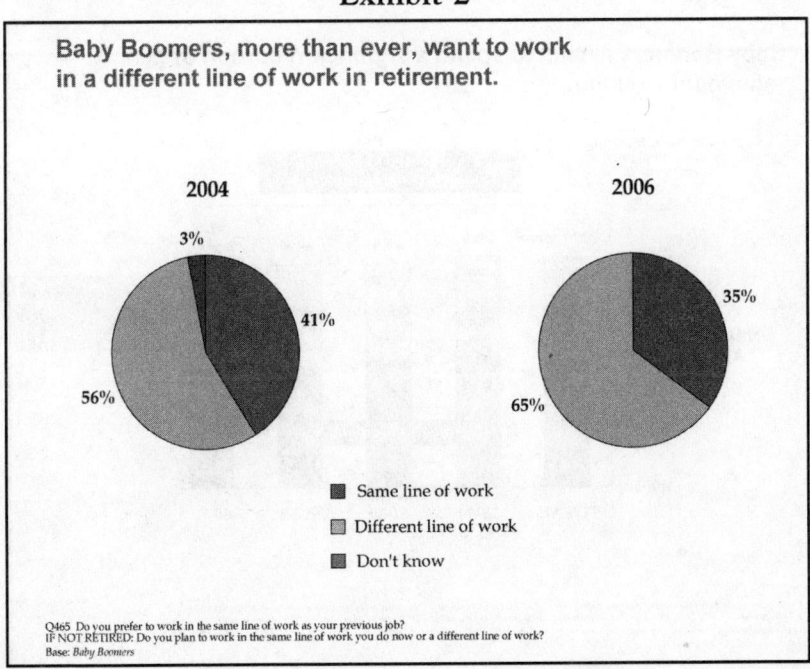

Exhibit 3

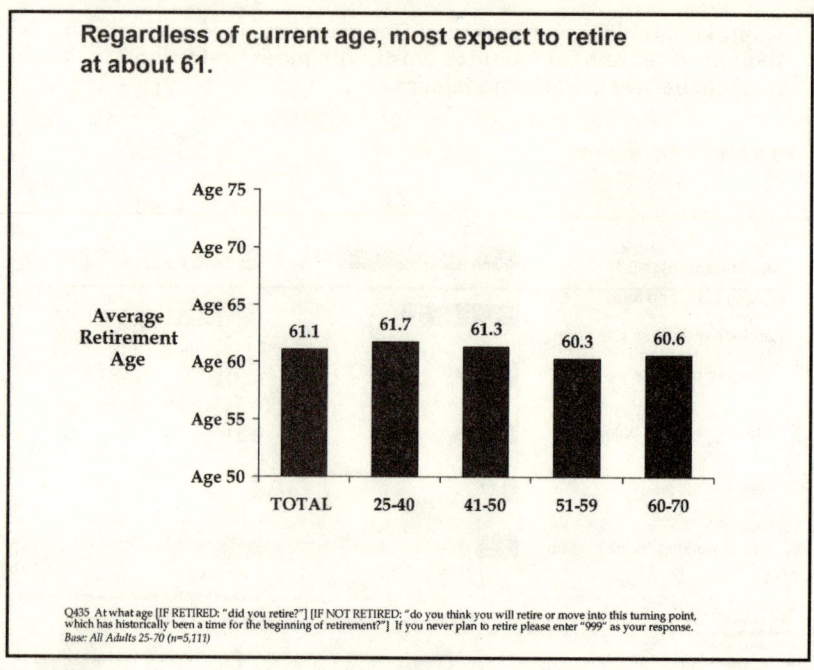

Exhibit 4

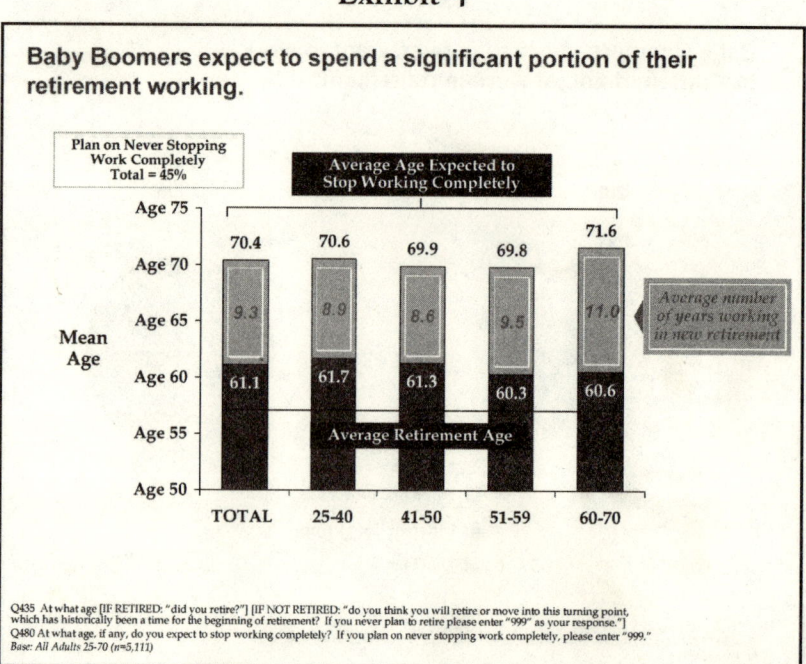

Exhibit 5

The 'New Retirement' is already well established among 60 to 70 year olds and among older Boomers. While a substantial proportion of this age group reports being retired, the majority of those retired are either working or say they will work but in a new work leisure balance.

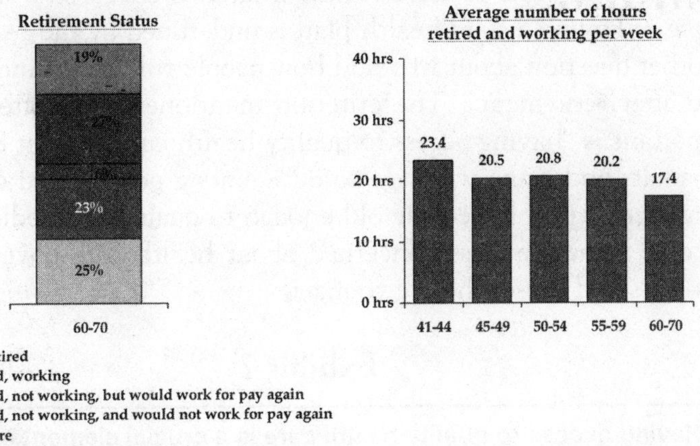

Retirement Status (60-70)
- 19% — Not retired (top)
- 27%
- 10% (approx)
- 23%
- 25%

☐ Not retired
■ Retired, working
☐ Retired, not working, but would work for pay again
■ Retired, not working, and would not work for pay again
■ Not sure

Average number of hours retired and working per week
- 41-44: 23.4
- 45-49: 20.5
- 50-54: 20.8
- 55-59: 20.2
- 60-70: 17.4

Q 415 Which of the following best describes you?
Base: All Adults 25-70 (n=5,111)
Q410 How many hours per week do you work, on average?
Base: Retired and working
Q 430 Do you think you will ever work for pay again?
Base: Retired and not working

Source: Merrill Lynch / AgeWave / Harris Interactive

Exhibit 6

Continuing To Work Is Not Only About The Money

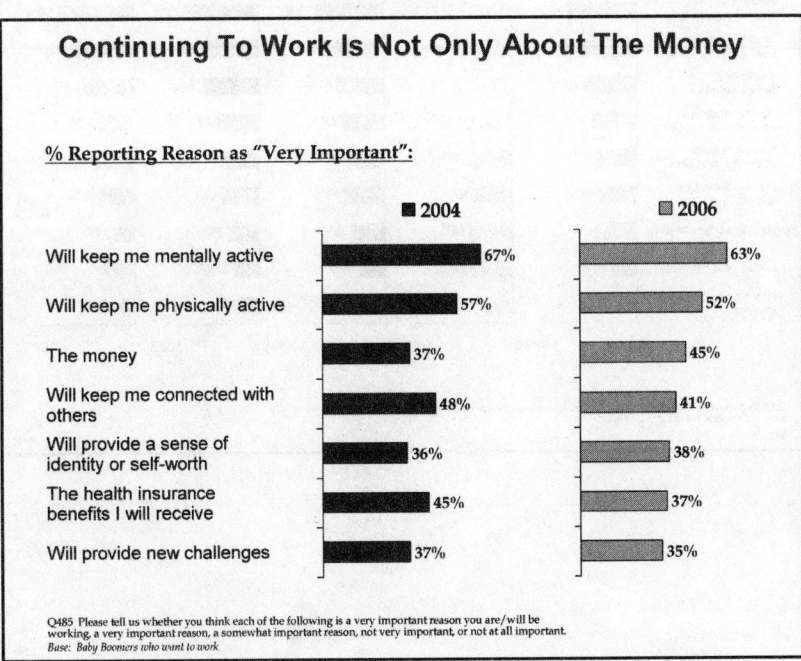

% Reporting Reason as "Very Important":

Reason	2004	2006
Will keep me mentally active	67%	63%
Will keep me physically active	57%	52%
The money	37%	45%
Will keep me connected with others	48%	41%
Will provide a sense of identity or self-worth	36%	38%
The health insurance benefits I will receive	45%	37%
Will provide new challenges	37%	35%

Q485 Please tell us whether you think each of the following is a very important reason you are/will be working, a very important reason, a somewhat important reason, not very important, or not at all important.
Base: Baby Boomers who want to work

2. Concerns About Access to Health Care and Coverage in Later Life

Exhibit 7 showed that many Baby Boomers expect to work later in their lives in order to have health insurance coverage. The importance of having a solid health plan is underlined by the responses to another question about why and how people will determine where to live after retirement. The criterion mentioned most often as very important is "having access to quality health care" (given by 74% of all adults and rising with age to 80% among people aged 60 to 70). However, as people become old enough to qualify for Medicare, they become somewhat less concerned about health care coverage than Boomers and those who are younger.

Exhibit 7

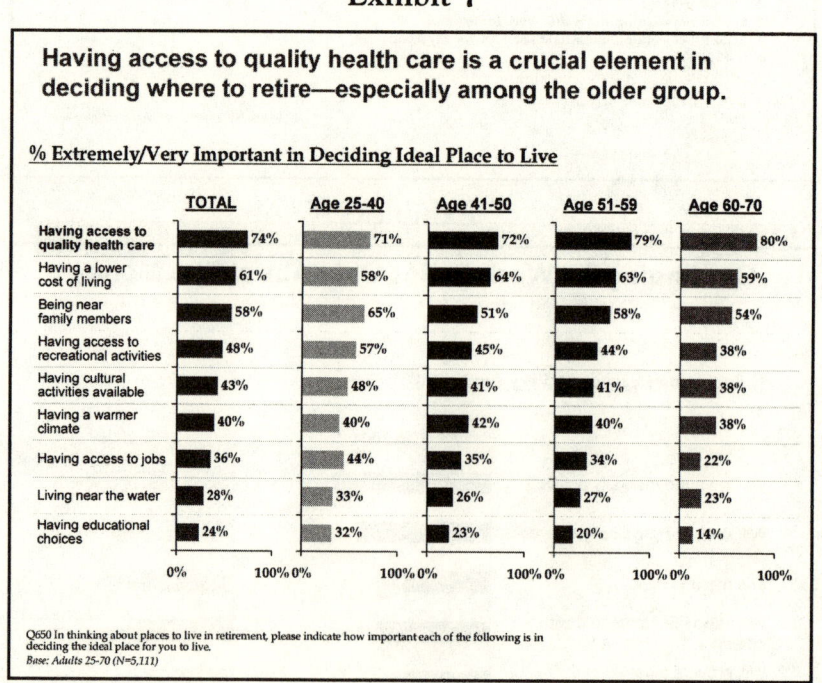

Having access to quality health care is a crucial element in deciding where to retire—especially among the older group.

% Extremely/Very Important in Deciding Ideal Place to Live

	TOTAL	Age 25-40	Age 41-50	Age 51-59	Age 60-70
Having access to quality health care	74%	71%	72%	79%	80%
Having a lower cost of living	61%	58%	64%	63%	59%
Being near family members	58%	65%	51%	58%	54%
Having access to recreational activities	48%	57%	45%	44%	38%
Having cultural activities available	43%	48%	41%	41%	38%
Having a warmer climate	40%	40%	42%	40%	38%
Having access to jobs	36%	44%	35%	34%	22%
Living near the water	28%	33%	26%	27%	23%
Having educational choices	24%	32%	23%	20%	14%

Q650 In thinking about places to live in retirement, please indicate how important each of the following is in deciding the ideal place for you to live.
Base: Adults 25-70 (N=5,111)

Exhibit 8

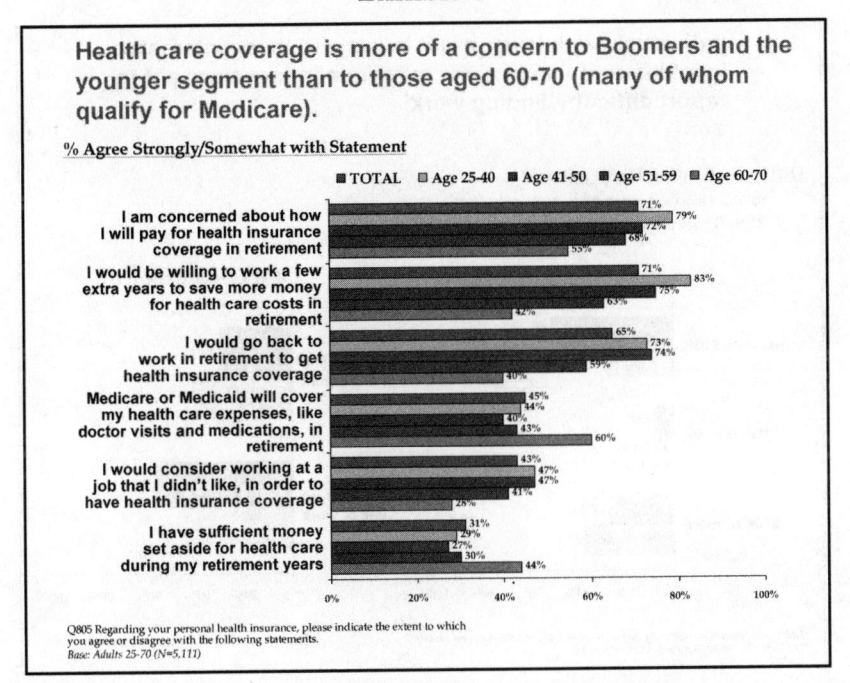

Health care coverage is more of a concern to Boomers and the younger segment than to those aged 60-70 (many of whom qualify for Medicare).

% Agree Strongly/Somewhat with Statement

■ TOTAL ☐ Age 25-40 ■ Age 41-50 ■ Age 51-59 ■ Age 60-70

Statement	TOTAL	Age 25-40	Age 41-50	Age 51-59	Age 60-70
I am concerned about how I will pay for health insurance coverage in retirement	71%	79%	72%	68%	55%
I would be willing to work a few extra years to save more money for health care costs in retirement	71%	83%	75%	63%	42%
I would go back to work in retirement to get health insurance coverage	65%	73%	74%	59%	40%
Medicare or Medicaid will cover my health care expenses, like doctor visits and medications, in retirement	45%	44%	40%	43%	60%
I would consider working at a job that I didn't like, in order to have health insurance coverage	43%	47%	47%	41%	28%
I have sufficient money set aside for health care during my retirement years	31%	29%	27%	30%	44%

Q805 Regarding your personal health insurance, please indicate the extent to which you agree or disagree with the following statements.
Base: Adults 25-70 (N=5,111)

3. Older People Who Need to Work the Most Have the Most Difficulty Finding Work

Unfortunately, older workers with fewer financial assets have more difficulty finding work than people with greater financial resources. This surely reflects the fact that older people with more job skills, or who held more senior positions when they were younger, are more likely to have the kind of talents that are attractive to employers.

In our research among people aged 60 or older who wanted to work, fully 50 percent of those with financial assets of less than $25,000 reported having difficulty finding work. Among those with assets of $75,000 or more, only 27 percent said they had difficulty finding work.

Those and other findings in our research suggest that the gap between those who will be well prepared financially for their later years and those who are not well prepared is likely to widen as the former find paid work later in life and many of the others fail to do so.

Exhibit 9

Individuals with lower asset levels and those interested in a 'different line of work' in retirement are more apt to report difficulty finding work.

Difficulty Finding Work After 60
- ■ Yes, I have had difficulty finding work
- □ No, I have not had difficulty finding work

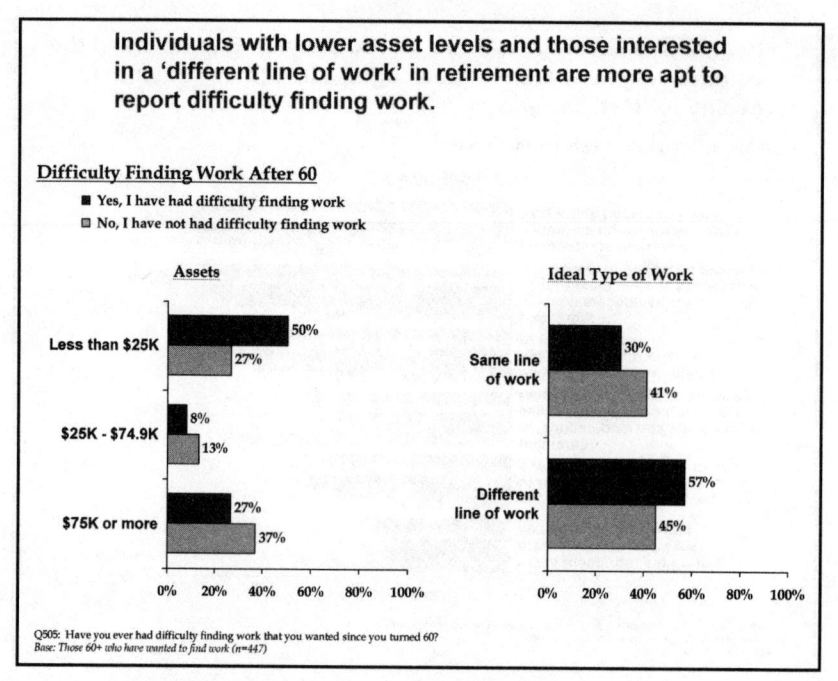

Assets
- Less than $25K: 50% / 27%
- $25K - $74.9K: 8% / 13%
- $75K or more: 27% / 37%

Ideal Type of Work
- Same line of work: 30% / 41%
- Different line of work: 57% / 45%

Q505: Have you ever had difficulty finding work that you wanted since you turned 60?
Base: Those 60+ who have wanted to find work (n=447)

4. Priorities of HR Directors

Obviously the employment of older workers depends on supply and demand–how many qualified older people are willing and able to work, and how much employers need workers. Human Resource managers have many tasks and priorities. Key questions that we sought to address were how HR directors view older workers and how much importance they attach to recruiting, motivating, and retaining them.

The research found that only a quarter of HR directors in large and medium-sized companies were "very concerned" about the large number of Baby Boomers approaching retirement. Only 5 percent reported that the retirement of Baby Boomers is a top priority issue for them; however, half (53%) said that it was an important issue for them but not a top priority. These views of HR directors were very similar to their perceptions of their senior managers' concerns.

When shown a list of ten potential issues, HR directors were most likely to see the rising cost of benefit programs as a serious problem. Second on their list of perceived problems was recruiting, training and retaining *younger* workers (68%). Retaining older workers came bottom of the list (38%). However, most HR directors told us that retaining skilled labor (68%) and the brain drain from people who leave (60%) were serious problems for their organizations; and, of course, many older workers have the skills and abilities that their employers want to retain.

Exhibit 10

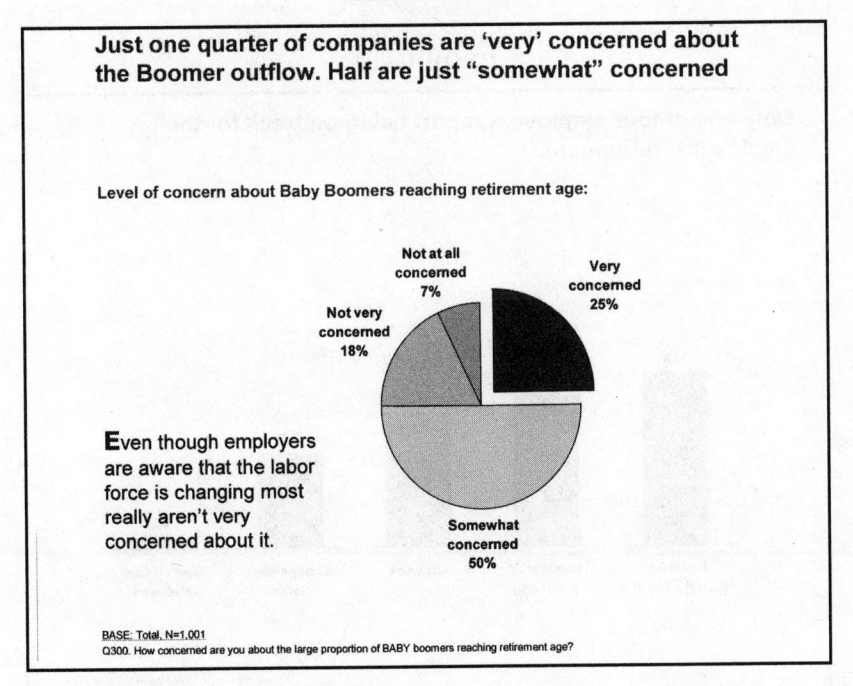

Just one quarter of companies are 'very' concerned about the Boomer outflow. Half are just "somewhat" concerned

Level of concern about Baby Boomers reaching retirement age:

- Not at all concerned 7%
- Not very concerned 18%
- Very concerned 25%
- Somewhat concerned 50%

Even though employers are aware that the labor force is changing most really aren't very concerned about it.

BASE: Total, N=1,001
Q300. How concerned are you about the large proportion of BABY boomers reaching retirement age?

5. HR Directors' Attitudes and Expectations

Most employers have done relatively little to prepare for the large number of Baby Boomers who will soon reach retirement age. Only a quarter (24%) of HR directors reported that their companies were "on track" in their preparations.

One hypothetical solution to the labor shortages that may be created by Baby Boomers leaving the workforce is to outsource their work overseas to countries such as China or India. The great majority (70%) of employers did not think this would help them at all. However, almost half of manufacturers (48%) see outsourcing as at least a partial solution to their looming skills shortage problems.

As employers view increasing shortages, they anticipate that the greatest impact will be a shortage of highly skilled professionals (35%) and middle management (24%).

Many employers (40%) believe their employees would value more health coverage than any other benefit. These perceptions are on target. Large numbers of people of all ages reported that they were concerned about how they would pay for health insurance in retirement.

Exhibit 11

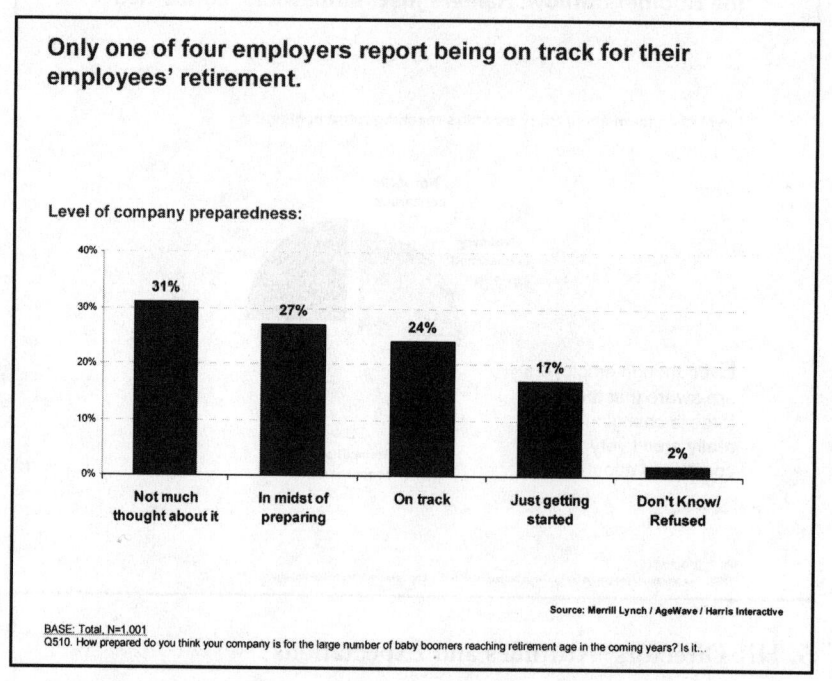

Only one of four employers report being on track for their employees' retirement.

Level of company preparedness:

- Not much thought about it: 31%
- In midst of preparing: 27%
- On track: 24%
- Just getting started: 17%
- Don't Know/Refused: 2%

Source: Merrill Lynch / AgeWave / Harris Interactive
BASE: Total, N=1,001
Q510. How prepared do you think your company is for the large number of baby boomers reaching retirement age in the coming years? Is it...

Exhibit 12

Outsourcing is generally not viewed as a solution to labor shortages; but many manufacturing companies believe it is.

Extent overseas outsourcing will be used to deal with staff and labor shortages:

	Total	Mfg	Whl/Retail	Services	Fin/Ins/RE	Other
	1001	200	193	284	218	106
	%	%	%	%	%	%
A great extent	5	13	2	4	4	0
Somewhat	9	18	**48%** 7	4	14	7
A little	14	17	17	11	14	14
Not at all	70	51	73	78	64	76
Don't Know/Refused	2	2	2	3	4	2

Half of manufacturing firms are likely to consider outsourcing as a solution (compared to 25% of employers in other industries)

BASE: Total, N=1,001, Mfg. N=200; Whl/Retail, N=193; Services, N=284; Fin/Ins/RE, N=218; Other, N=106
Q620. To what extent will your company be able to deal with looming staff and labor shortages by outsourcing work overseas?

Exhibit 13

Many employers believe that providing more/better Healthcare is the key to retaining older workers and employees agree.

Employers believe employees would value more health coverage more than any other benefit such as increased compensation, flex scheduling and more vacation. This is aligned with employee views—71% are concerned about how they will pay for health insurance during retirement and two-thirds would continue working just to get coverage

Most appealing benefits:

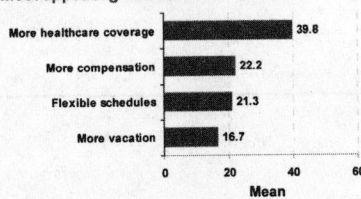

Benefit	Mean
More healthcare coverage	39.8
More compensation	22.2
Flexible schedules	21.3
More vacation	16.7

Agree strongly/somewhat... By Age (25-40, 41-50, 51-59, 60-70)

Statement	25-40	41-50	51-59	60-70
I am concerned about how I will pay for health insurance coverage in retirement	79%	72%	68%	55%
I would be willing to work a few extra years to save more money for health care costs in retirement	83%	75%	63%	42%
I would go back to work in retirement to get health insurance coverage	73%	74%	59%	40%
Medicare or Medicaid will cover my health care expenses, like doctor visits and medications, in retirement	44%	40%	43%	60%
I would consider working at a job that I didn't like, in order to have health insurance coverage	47%	47%	41%	28%
I have sufficient money set aside for health care during my retirement years	29%	27%	30%	44%

BASE: Total, N=964 (respondents who answered 3 or more comparisons)
Q625. Suppose your company gave your older employee the option to trade off benefits against each other. I am going to read several pairs of benefits that may or may not be appealing to your older workers. For each pair, please tell me which one would be more appealing to your older employees.

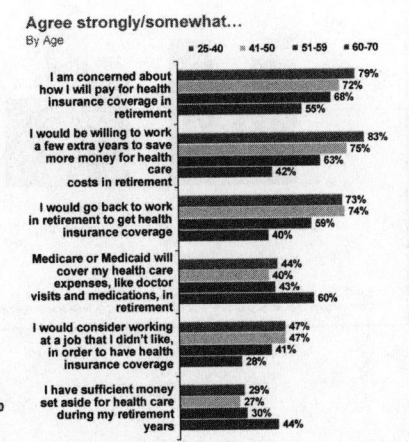

BASE: All Adults 25-70 (n=5,111)
Q805 Regarding your personal health insurance, please indicate the extent to which you agree or disagree with the following statements.

6. What Companies Are and Are Not Doing

Our research shows how little most corporate employers are doing to retain their older workers. The steps the largest number told us they were taking were retirement counseling (46%), the introduction of flextime (44%), and allowing employees to pursue other interests (42%). Most employers are not doing much more than this.

Most employers don't take action to deal with potential problems until they become very concerned about them, and most are not. Unsurprisingly, our research found that employers who were concerned about the Boomer outflow were much more likely to be taking action to deal with the problems than those who were not concerned.

Exhibit 14

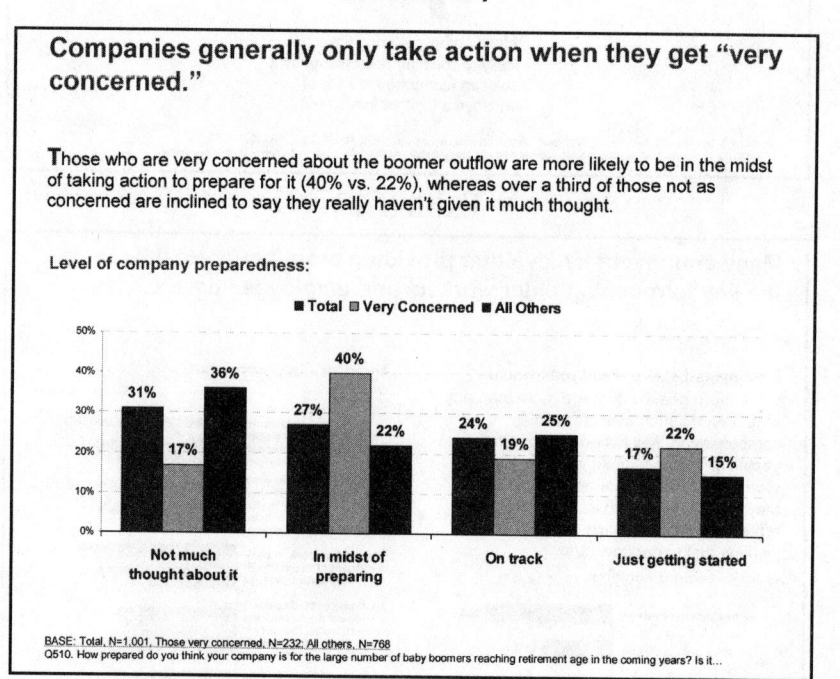

Companies generally only take action when they get "very concerned."

Those who are very concerned about the boomer outflow are more likely to be in the midst of taking action to prepare for it (40% vs. 22%), whereas over a third of those not as concerned are inclined to say they really haven't given it much thought.

Level of company preparedness:

■ Total ☐ Very Concerned ■ All Others

	Total	Very Concerned	All Others
Not much thought about it	31%	17%	36%
In midst of preparing	27%	40%	22%
On track	24%	19%	25%
Just getting started	17%	22%	15%

BASE: Total, N=1,001. Those very concerned, N=232; All others, N=768
Q510. How prepared do you think your company is for the large number of baby boomers reaching retirement age in the coming years? Is it...

7. This Is Also an Important Issue in Many Other Countries

The retirement revolution and the looming talent shortages resulting from the retirement of Baby Boomers will affect many other countries, not just the United States. This is particularly true of developed countries in Europe, Japan, and other industrialized countries. However, this is not true, or is less true, in poorer, developing countries, with higher birth rates and much larger numbers of young people.

The vision of retirement as "an opportunity for a whole new chapter in life" is most widespread in the richer countries in North America and Europe. The more traditional view of retirement as a time for rest and relaxation is most common in poor countries and those of intermediate wealth, particularly in Latin America, the Middle East, and Africa.

However, in all regions of the world, and in rich and poor countries, only small minorities view retirement as a time when they will never work for pay. (It should be noted that in poor countries with no state pension or social security system, particularly where the majority are peasant farmers, the concept of retirement scarcely exists. The assumption of most Indian and African farmers is that they will continue to work as long as they are capable of doing so).

While there are some global similarities, our international surveys have found large differences between different countries. Money is seen as the principal reason for working in later life in India, Russia, and Turkey. People in Poland and Sweden are the most likely to value "connecting with others," while people in Saudi Arabia, Egypt, and Malaysia are the most likely to value "having something meaningful to do" as a reason for working.

The public in all countries believes that there are many things employers could do to increase the likelihood that they would continue to work later in life. Although there are substantial differences between different countries and regions, many people would be attracted by employers who offer older workers the opportunity to guide and teach younger workers, to work fewer hours, and to learn new skills or do different types of work. However, many employees who would like their employers to offer these opportunities reported that they are not offered.

Exhibit 15

Worldwide – many view retirement positively; in the U.S./Canada, and to some extent Europe, retirement is viewed primarily as a new opportunity

	International Average (21469)	U.S./Canada (2055)	Europe (6930)	Latin America (2042)	Asia (8442)	Middle East/Africa (2000)
Not sure	3	2	2	—	3	5
An opportunity for a whole new chapter in life	32	61	37	19	28	14
A continuation of what life was	17	—	17	13	17	21
A time for rest and relaxation	40	12	35	51	45	47
The beginning of the end	9	3	8	13	8	13
	—	23	—	—	—	—

Base: Consumers
Q520. Which one of the following statements do you agree with most? Retirement is...
*Data is from 2004 for this question in Canada, U.S., Brazil, Mexico, France, UK, China, Hong Kong, India, Japan
*The regional numbers are averages for the countries surveyed, giving each country an equal weight

Source: HSBC / AgeWave / Harris Interactive

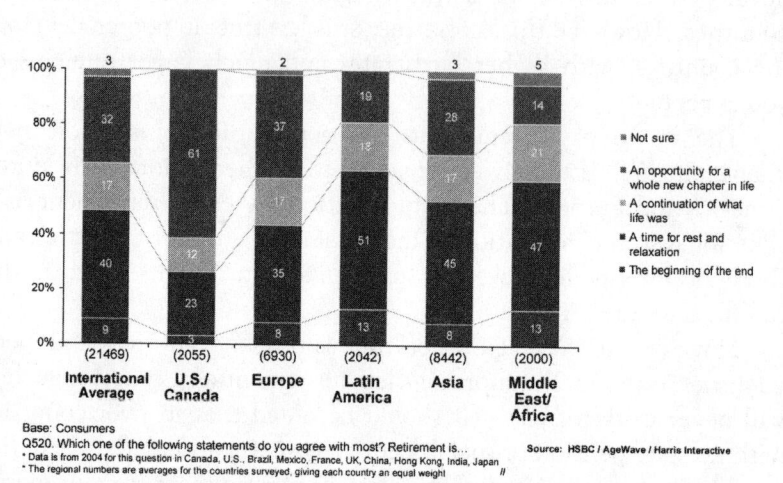

Exhibit 16

Richer countries are more likely to think that retirement is an opportunity for a whole new chapter in life

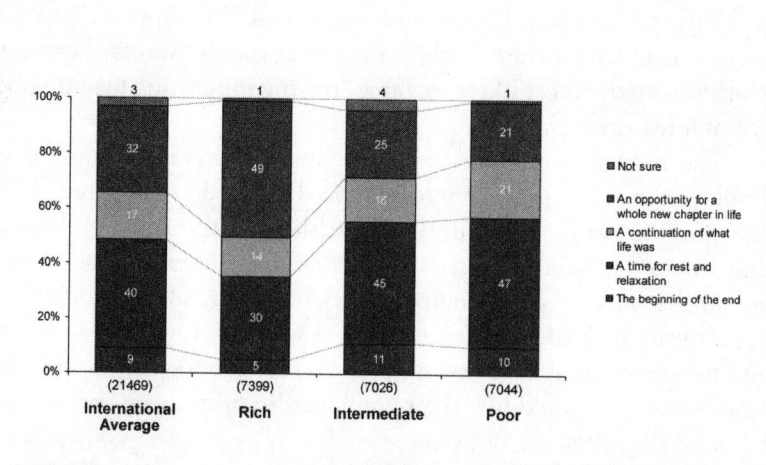

	International Average (21469)	Rich (7399)	Intermediate (7026)	Poor (7044)
Not sure	3	1	4	1
An opportunity for a whole new chapter in life	32	49	25	21
A continuation of what life was	17	14	16	21
A time for rest and relaxation	40	30	45	47
The beginning of the end	9	5	11	10

Base: Consumers
Q520. Which one of the following statements do you agree with most? Retirement is...
*Data is from 2004 for this question in Canada, U.S., Brazil, Mexico, France, UK, China, Hong Kong, India, Japan

Resources: HSBC / AgeWave / Harris Interactive

Increasing Workforce Participation Among Older Workers ▼ 35

Exhibit 17

Only a small minority would like to retire and stop working completely

Consistent throughout all regions

	International Average (21469) %	U.S./ Canada (2055) %	Europe (6930) %	Latin America (2042) %	Asia (8442) %	Middle East/ Africa (2000) %
Going back and forth between periods of work and leisure	47	50	41	64	46	53
Never working for pay again	20	19	22	12	23	15
Working part-time	19	19	21	16	20	9
Working full-time	9	10	10	9	7	10

Source: HSBC / AgeWave / Harris Interactive

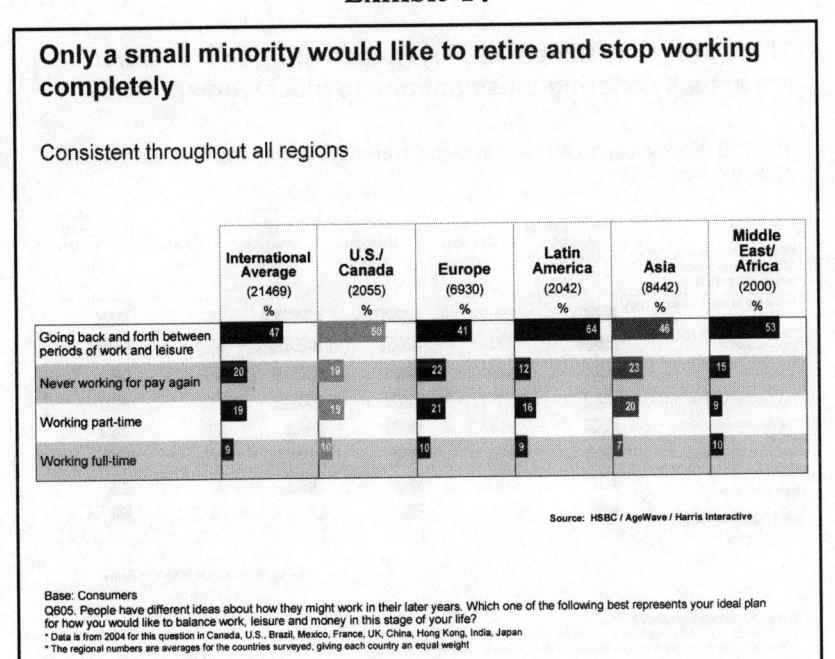

Base: Consumers
Q605. People have different ideas about how they might work in their later years. Which one of the following best represents your ideal plan for how you would like to balance work, leisure and money in this stage of your life?
* Data is from 2004 for this question in Canada, U.S., Brazil, Mexico, France, UK, China, Hong Kong, India, Japan
* The regional numbers are averages for the countries surveyed, giving each country an equal weight

Exhibit 18

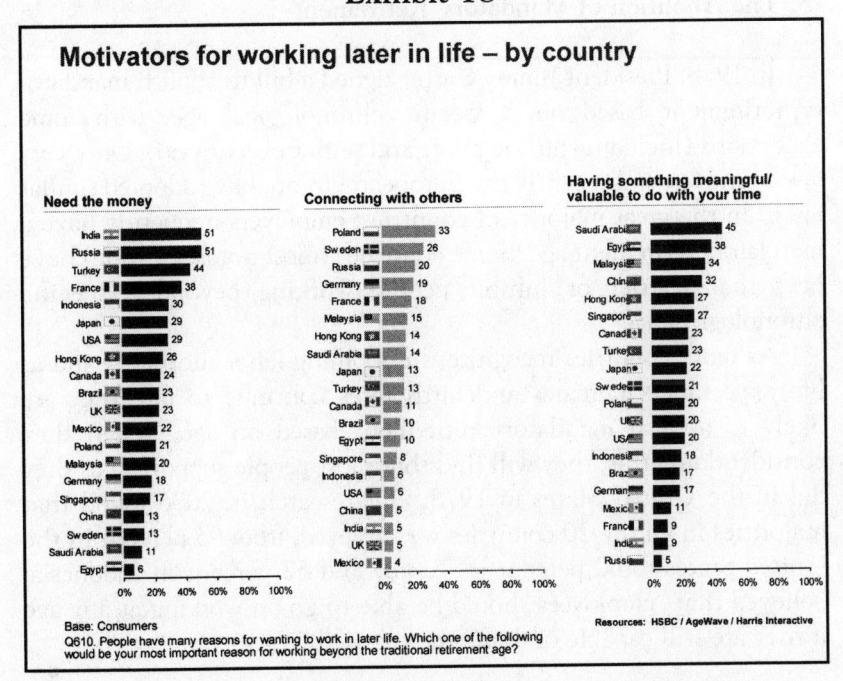

Motivators for working later in life – by country

Need the money
Country	%
India	51
Russia	51
Turkey	44
France	38
Indonesia	30
Japan	29
USA	29
Hong Kong	26
Canada	24
Brazil	23
UK	23
Mexico	22
Poland	21
Malaysia	20
Germany	18
Singapore	17
China	13
Sweden	13
Saudi Arabia	11
Egypt	6

Connecting with others
Country	%
Poland	33
Sweden	26
Russia	20
Germany	19
France	18
Malaysia	15
Hong Kong	14
Saudi Arabia	14
Japan	13
Turkey	13
Canada	11
Brazil	10
Egypt	10
Singapore	8
Indonesia	6
USA	6
China	5
India	5
UK	5
Mexico	4

Having something meaningful/ valuable to do with your time
Country	%
Saudi Arabia	45
Egypt	38
Malaysia	34
China	32
Hong Kong	27
Singapore	27
Canada	23
Turkey	23
Japan	22
Sweden	21
Poland	20
UK	20
USA	20
Indonesia	18
Brazil	17
Germany	17
Mexico	11
France	9
India	9
Russia	5

Resources: HSBC / AgeWave / Harris Interactive

Base: Consumers
Q610. People have many reasons for wanting to work in later life. Which one of the following would be your most important reason for working beyond the traditional retirement age?

Exhibit 19

There are many things employers can offer, but far fewer are actually offering these options to older workers

The U.S./Canada and Latin America are currently offering more options to older workers

What an employer <u>does</u> offer to make working more attractive	International Average (10933) %	U.S./ Canada (1125) %	Europe (3621) %	Latin America (895) %	Asia (4341) %	Middle East/ Africa (951) %
The ability to continue earning an income	43	79	50	60	26	32
The ability to guide and teach younger workers	39	55	39	53	30	41
An enjoyable and stimulating work place	33	61	35	51	21	17
The opportunity to learn new skills	32	54	35	48	20	29
The opportunity to work fewer hours	32	49	35	37	22	30
The ability to undertake less physically demanding work	31	44	29	45	25	32
New kinds of work	24	41	26	36	15	19
Not sure/Nothing	26	9	30	15	33	21

Source: HSBC / AgeWave / Harris Interactive

Base: All currently employed
Q617. Which of the following does your employer offer to those aged over 50?
* The regional numbers are averages for the countries surveyed, giving each country an equal weight

8. The Abolition of Mandatory Retirement

In 1978, President Jimmy Carter signed a bill to abolish mandatory retirement based on a specific chronological age, with some exceptions (including airline pilots and senior executives). Only very few countries, and recently the European Union, have adopted similar laws. In the great majority of countries, employers frequently have a mandatory retirement age. Some countries (most notably China) have laws that restrict or inhibit people working beyond a specific chronological age.

As more countries recognize the looming labor shortages, and as life expectancy increases and birth rates continue to fall, they are likely to abolish mandatory retirement based on age. When they consider doing this, they will find that most people support it–as they did in the United States in 1978. Our research in 2006 found that majorities in all the 20 countries we surveyed, from 93 percent in the United States to 60 percent in Turkey and 52 percent in Indonesia, believed that "employees should be able to go on working at any age if they are still capable of doing the job well."

Exhibit 20

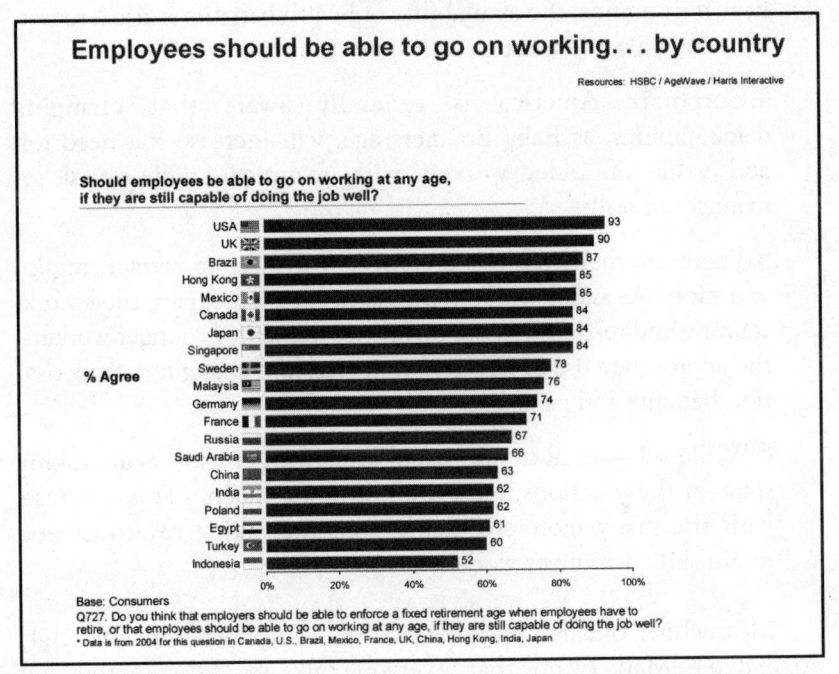

Employees should be able to go on working... by country

Resources: HSBC / AgeWave / Harris Interactive

Should employees be able to go on working at any age, if they are still capable of doing the job well?

% Agree

Country	%
USA	93
UK	90
Brazil	87
Hong Kong	85
Mexico	85
Canada	84
Japan	84
Singapore	84
Sweden	78
Malaysia	76
Germany	74
France	71
Russia	67
Saudi Arabia	66
China	63
India	62
Poland	62
Egypt	61
Turkey	60
Indonesia	52

Base: Consumers
Q727. Do you think that employers should be able to enforce a fixed retirement age when employees have to retire, or that employees should be able to go on working at any age, if they are still capable of doing the job well?
* Data is from 2004 for this question in Canada, U.S., Brazil, Mexico, France, UK, China, Hong Kong, India, Japan

In Conclusion

As we look to the future and the strong economic and social benefit of retaining qualified older workers in the labor force, employers and government should know and understand the following:

1. Retirement is not the same as ending work. Most people want and expect to remain in the workforce for almost ten years after what they think of as retirement. This is a global phenomenon that is not unique to the United States.

2. There are many reasons why so many people want, or expect, to work when they are relatively old. These reasons include money, but work is also seen as stimulating mental and physical well-being, keeping people socially connected, providing a sense of self-worth, and providing new challenges.

3. In the United States, unlike countries that provide universal health insurance, the availability of health benefits is also a reason why many people want to work later in life.

4. Corporate America is generally aware that changing demographics, as Baby Boomers age, will increase the need for, and value of, older workers with technical, professional, or managerial skills.

5. There are many actions employers can take to attract, retain, and motivate older workers including flex-time, part-time work, training and re-training, opportunities to mentor younger workers, the appropriate use of new technologies, and changing compensation benefits and packages.

6. While substantial minorities of American employers are taking some of these actions, most are not doing much. This contrasts with the many more steps employers are taking to attract and retain skilled younger workers.

Meanwhile, one is reminded of the saying (often but wrongly attributed to Mark Twain) that "everyone talks about the weather, but nobody does anything about it." A growing number of corporate managers are talking about how to retain talented older workers, but much more action needs to be taken as we face growing talent shortages.

Live Longer, Work Longer:
An OECD Perspective on Ageing and Employment Policies in the United States[*]

John P. Martin

Director for Employment, Labour, and Social Affairs, Organisation for Economic Co-operation and Development (OECD), Paris-based with 30 member countries

Introduction

Older people offer tremendous potential value to businesses, the economy, and society. Unfortunately, they often represent an untapped and discriminated-against resource, as many public policy measures and workplace practices pose serious barriers to older workers continuing to work or create strong incentives to retire early. Many of these policies and practices are relics from a bygone era and are no longer sustainable in an era of rapid population ageing, which is placing strains on public finances and putting downward pressure on the growth in living standards. Thus, there is a need to look beyond traditional stereotypes about ageing in order to benefit from the growing numbers of older citizens, many of whom would, in fact, choose to work longer given appropriate incentives, policies, and workplace practices.

The OECD has reported extensively on public pension and early retirement systems and the need for reforms of these systems to cope with population ageing.[1] As part of these reforms, financial incentives to remain longer in work must be strengthened, including removing disincentives in other welfare schemes and private pension arrangements that may be acting as alternative and publicly-subsidised pathways to early retirement. However, this may not be enough to encourage later retirement. Older people also need to be provided

---

[*] I am very grateful to my colleagues Mark Keese and Pascal Marianna for all their help in preparing this paper. The views expressed are my own and should not be held to represent those of the OCED or its member governments.

with better job opportunities. This will require a range of measures to be taken by government, employers, and trade unions to: adapt wage-setting practices to ageing workforces; tackle age discrimination; improve the job skills and working conditions of older workers; and provide better employment services for older job seekers. In addition, older workers will need to change their own attitudes towards working longer and acquiring new skills.

Relatively little is known about what OECD countries have been, or should be, doing, to improve job opportunities for older workers. Therefore, over the four-year period from 2001 to 2005, the OECD undertook a thematic review of policies to improve the labour market prospects for older workers.[2] Altogether, 21 countries participated in the review including the United States (see Box 1). This paper summarises the main lessons and policy recommendations from the U.S. report in the light of the experiences of other OECD countries. Section 1 highlights some of the main stylised facts concerning population ageing and the workforce. Section 2 sets out the key policy directions that OECD countries are taking to encourage older workers to remain active longer. The third section provides some concrete examples of what reforms OECD countries have put in place or are planning to implement to further this objective. The final section summarises the main recommendations in our U.S. report.

Box 1. The OECD's project on "Ageing and Employment Policies"

The series of country reviews of policies to improve the labour market prospects of older workers was begun in 2001 and completed in 2005. 21 countries participated in the review: Australia, Austria, Belgium, Canada, the Czech Republic, Denmark, Finland, France, Germany, Ireland, Italy, Japan, Korea, Luxembourg, the Netherlands, Norway, Spain, Sweden, Switzerland, the United Kingdom, and the United States. For each country, a separate report was published: the U.S. report was published as OECD (2005). Each country report contains a review of labour market trends for older workers, a survey of the main disincentives and barriers to employment for older workers, an assessment of the adequacy of existing measures to overcome these disincentives and barriers, and a set of policy recommendations for further action by the public authorities, employers, workers, and unions.

OECD (2006a) provides a synthesis of the main lessons which emerged from the 21 country reports.

For more details, see
www.OECD.ORG/ELS/EMPLOYMENT/Older Workers

1. The Key Stylised Facts Concerning Ageing Populations and Workforces

It is well-known that all OECD countries are experiencing population ageing as a result of both a steep drop in fertility rates and an increase in longevity. However, this is more pronounced and occurring at a faster pace in some countries than in others. For example, Figure 1 shows that by 2050, more than one-third of the population is projected to be aged 65 and over in Italy, Japan, Korea, and Spain compared with around one-fifth or less in Mexico, Turkey, and the United States. Indeed, in some crucial respects, the United States is better placed than many OECD countries to cope with population ageing. Thanks mainly to a relatively high fertility rate and high net immigration (both legal and illegal), its population is projected to age less rapidly over the period to 2050 than in most other OECD countries.

Figure 1 Population ageing is occuring in all OECD countries but less rapidly in the U.S.

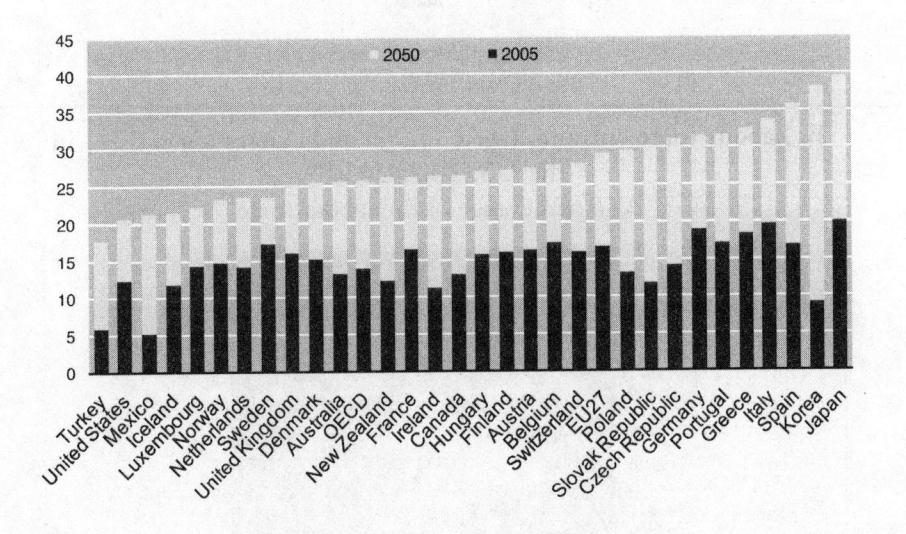

But there is no room for complacency. Figure 2 (Panel A) shows that U.S. labour force growth is projected to slow significantly over the period to 2050. Panel B shows that the projected number of workers retiring will rise relative to the number of new entrants. These trends, in turn, are likely to result in slower economic growth, rising skill shortages, and strong pressures on public finances.

Figure 2. No room for complacency

A. Labour force growth, 1950-2050*
Annual average % change

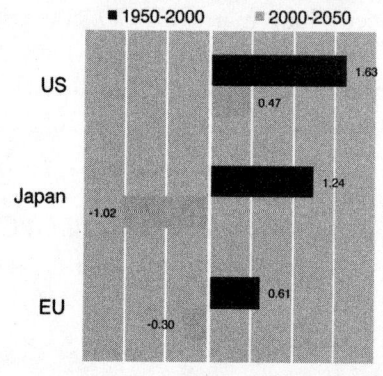

■ 1950-2000   ■ 2000-2050

Region	1950-2000	2000-2050
US	1.63	0.47
Japan	1.24	-1.02
EU	0.61	-0.30

B. Labour force entrants (aged 15-29) and exiters (aged 50+) in the US, 2005-2050*
As a percentage of the labour force

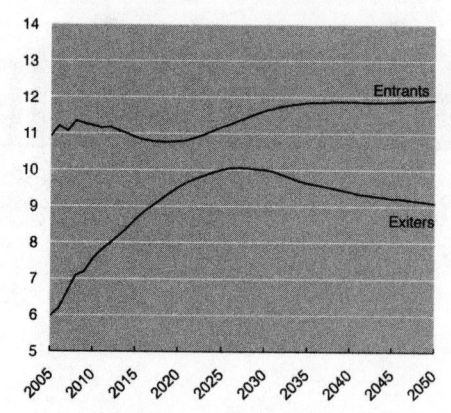

* Assuming labour force entry and exit behavior by age and gender remain unchanged.

Research by the OECD and many other organisations including the Congressional Budget Office shows that encouraging older workers to remain longer in the workplace would clearly help to boost economic growth and reduce the burden of future public spending on Social Security and Medicare. On this front, there is also good news for the United States. Figure 3 shows that, compared with many other OECD countries, a high proportion of older Americans are working, and this rate has increased over the past 10 years. But again, complacency is not in order. Many OECD countries have higher employment rates of older workers than the United States and early retirement, while not as endemic as in some European countries, is nevertheless a fairly frequent event in the United States. The Social Security system is a major determinant of early retirement in the United States, with a pronounced impact between the ages of 62 and 65.

Figure 3. To meet these challenges, employment at an older age must be encouraged, not discouraged

Percentage of older people aged 50 to 64 years who are employed, 2006

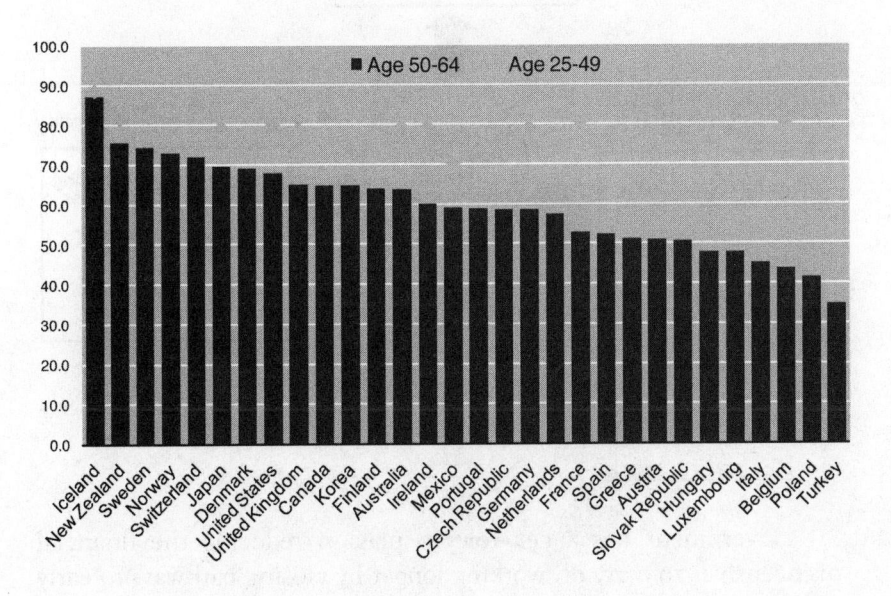

2. Policy Directions to Encourage Working Longer

An effective policy strategy to encourage older workers to carry on working has to address the full range of factors that are either pushing older workers out of work or pulling them into early retirement; it also has to involve all the key actors. The OECD's preferred strategy rests on three pillars (Figure 4): (i) rewarding work; (ii) changing employer practices; and (iii) improving employability. The rest of this section discusses each of these pillars in turn and provides examples of recent reforms undertaken by OECD countries in each area.

Figure 4. Key policy directions OECD countries are taking to encourage working longer

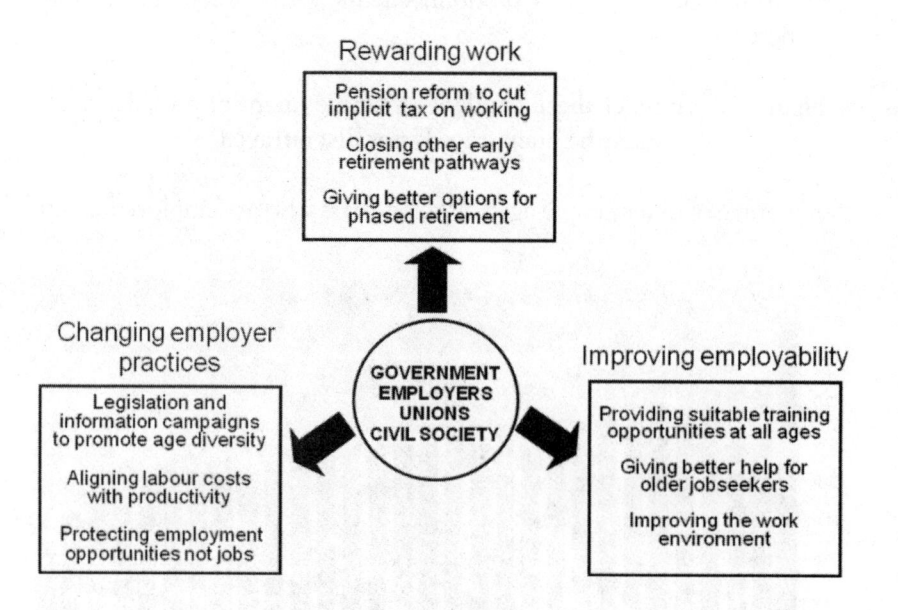

Rewarding work
- Pension reform to cut implicit tax on working
- Closing other early retirement pathways
- Giving better options for phased retirement

Changing employer practices
- Legislation and information campaigns to promote age diversity
- Aligning labour costs with productivity
- Protecting employment opportunities not jobs

GOVERNMENT EMPLOYERS UNIONS CIVIL SOCIETY

Improving employability
- Providing suitable training opportunities at all ages
- Giving better help for older jobseekers
- Improving the work environment

a. <u>Rewarding work</u>

Government has a key role to play in reducing the financial disincentives to carry on working longer by closing pathways to early retirement, raising the pension age, rewarding work at older ages, and allowing flexibility in combining income from work and pensions so that the older worker is financially better off as a result.

As OECD (2007) makes clear, there has been much action over the past two decades on the pension reform front (see Table A in the Appendix). There are several common features:
- Higher pension eligibility age for men and women (e.g. Denmark, Germany, Italy, Japan, Korea, U.S.) or for women alone (e.g. Australia, U.K.)
- Improved incentives to delay retirement (e.g. Australia, France, Germany, Italy, U.K.)
- Tighter qualifying conditions for retirement (e.g. France, Italy)
- Links to life expectancy and/or financial sustainability:
    - in earnings-related schemes (e.g. Germany, Japan)
    - in qualifying conditions (e.g. France)
    - through national accounts (e.g. Italy, Poland, Sweden)
    - through defined-contribution schemes (e.g. Australia, Hungary, Mexico, Poland, Slovakia, Sweden)
- Direct cuts in generosity:
    - lower accrual rates (e.g. Austria, Japan, Korea)

Figure 5. Effective age of retirement for men and the official age, 2000-2005

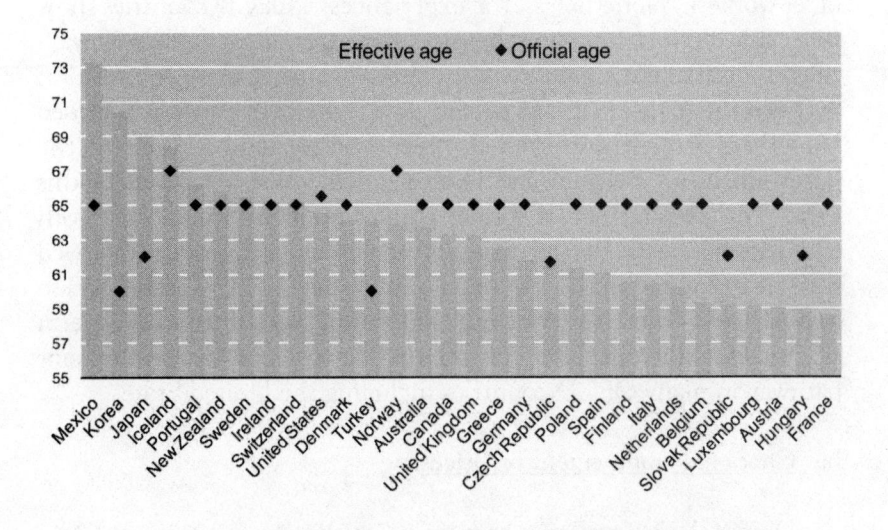

Despite the intense pension reform activity, it has to be noted that many of the reforms are often phased in slowly in order to sell them to voters and early retirement often remains possible via other workplace benefits, notably long-term sickness and disability benefits and unemployment benefits (see below). As a result, Figure 5 shows that the average effective retirement age is well below the official (or statutory) retirement age in many OECD countries, though the gap is not large in the United States.

One especially noteworthy trend in reform is to link pension benefits and entitlements to rising life expectancy or projected financial sustainability of the pension system. Table 1 shows that over the past two decades, 13 OECD countries have instituted such reforms. One prediction I would make is that over the next 10-15 years, many more OECD countries will introduce such a link in their pension systems, faced with rising life expectancy and the imperative need to encourage older workers to carry on working.

Another noteworthy trend, especially in Europe, is to either close down or restrict access greatly to formal early retirement schemes, or seek to tighten access to other pathways to early retirement via long-term sickness/disability benefits or unemployment benefits for older workers. Nonetheless, the experiences of OECD countries show that, unless reform is <u>comprehensive</u>, covering all available pathways to early retirement simultaneously, there is a real risk of substitution between them, i.e., as access to one early retirement pathway is closed but others are left unrestricted, older workers tend to shift to the latter schemes. Belgium and France provide clear examples of this risk: The phasing out of formal early retirement schemes in both countries has been offset by a rise in the numbers of older unemployed who are exempt from the requirement that they should search for a job actively in order to continue receiving benefits. Long-term sickness/disability benefits continue to be a major early-retirement pathway in many OECD countries including the United States.

b. <u>Changing employment practices</u>

Dismantling employer barriers to hiring and retaining older workers requires action by government, employers, and unions. Some countries have sought to deal with negative employer attitudes through age-discrimination legislation. Others have preferred to rely on public-information campaigns and guidelines. However, both approaches should be pursued. There also needs to be a better match between the costs of employing older workers and their productivity. And the appropriate balance needs to be found between protecting jobs of older workers and enhancing their labour mobility.

This part of the strategy to encourage older workers to keep working longer is proving to be the most difficult to put into practice effectively across all 21 OECD countries covered in our review. It seems that "ageism" is alive and well in most workplaces. Nor is anti-age discrimination legislation the answer. The U.S. led the OECD countries on this front when it first passed the Age Discrimination in Employment Act (ADEA) in 1967. Since then, most OECD countries have introduced similar legislation, with the notable exception of Japan.

Unfortunately, there are very few rigorous evaluations of the effects of anti-age discrimination legislation, and almost none outside the United States. OECD (2005) surveys the limited U.S. evaluation literature and concludes that there is "reasonably good evidence that this legislation (ADEA) increased retention of workers over age of 60." But it admits that there is much less evidence that ADEA has had any measurable impact on the hiring of older workers.

Employers need to be told not just what they cannot do, but they should also be informed and convinced of the benefits of having an age-diverse workplace. Several OECD countries (e.g. Finland, the Netherlands, U.K. and, most recently, France) have invested heavily in major public information campaigns to tackle ageism in the workplace. In some cases this has included guidelines for employers in terms of good conduct or good practices, as well as a general campaign to raise awareness among employers and the general public of issues related to population ageing and work. One well-known example is Finland's National Programme on Ageing Workers, which ran from 1998 to 2002 before it was succeeded by another programme called VETO (see Box 2). Various studies suggest that these Finnish programmes played some part in the very large increase over the past decade in employment rates for older workers in Finland, in addition to the effects of strong economic growth and pension/early retirement reforms: The employment rate for those aged 55-64 rose from 33.5 percent in 1994 to 54.5 percent in 2006.

> **Box 2. Finland's Information Campaigns to support longer working lives**
>
> Shortly after the end of the economic recession in the mid 1990s, a series of government programmes were introduced in Finland (OECD, 2004e). These focus on improving workability and working conditions in order to promote longer working lives.
>
> **The National Programme on Ageing Workers**
>
> This largest and best known of Finland's public programmes for older workers sought to improve employment opportunities and the workability of people over the age of 45, both those in work and the unemployed. Proposed by a special committee in 1996, the programme ran from 1998 to 2002. It was implemented jointly by the Ministry of Social Affairs and Health, the Ministry of Labour, and the Ministry of Education. The focus of the programme varied over time. In the initial phase, most measures concentrated on legislative amendments and information campaigns. The middle phase involved research and development projects, while the final phase focused on management training and development in the workplace.
>
> **The Well-Being at Work Programme**
>
> This programme, which ran from 2000 to 2003, operated at four levels: information provision and promotion of good practice; research and utilisation of research findings; support and funding for development projects; and monitoring of legislation. The main goal was to encourage people to stay in work longer.
>
> **The Workplace Development Programme**
>
> Launched in 1996 by the Ministry of Labour together with the social partners, this programme provides expert support to workplaces striving to improve the quality of working life. The programme has been extended beyond its original end date of 2003.
>
> **The VETO programme**
>
> This programme was introduced by the Ministry of Social Affairs and Health in 2003. Based on the experiences of the previous programmes, it sought to ensure that people could fully participate in working life, encouraged workers to stay on longer, and addressed job quality. The programme ran until 2007.

At the same time, one barrier that may discourage employers from hiring or retaining older workers is that they cost too much relative to their actual or expected productivity, though a partial offset may come from lower absenteeism and turnover among older workers in certain sectors. The too-high costs may reflect high "seniority-type" wages and/or high non-wage labour costs. One topical example of the latter is the high cost of employer-provided health insurance in the United States.

Few countries where wages rise steeply with age have tried directly to alter wage-setting practices in the private sector to tilt demand in favour of older workers. Japan and Korea, two countries where seniority wages have traditionally been very important, are the main exceptions, but moving away from pay based on seniority/age to one based more on performance is a very slow process.

Instead, many countries have introduced various types of wage subsidies that ultimately are designed to align labour costs for older workers more closely with their productivity. In some countries, this has been though a special wage subsidy scheme that may be targeted at older workers or may include older workers (sometimes with special or more generous eligibility conditions) as one of several target groups. In other countries, it has been through a reduction in employer Social Security contributions.

However, wage subsidy and job-creation schemes that are predominantly targeted on older workers raise a number of issues in terms of their effectiveness. First, they may involve substantial deadweight loss (i.e., a large proportion of subsidised workers would have been employed even without the subsidy) and substitution/displacement effects (i.e., subsidised jobs for eligible workers lead to the loss of jobs or job opportunities for other groups of workers ineligible for the subsidy). Therefore, wage subsidies that are targeted on age alone, such as some of the schemes in Austria and Korea, risk being quite blunt instruments and may result in small net employment effects at considerable cost to the public purse. Second, subsidies for older workers as a group may lead to stigmatisation and reinforce negative attitudes on the part of employers to hiring and retaining older workers. Thus, a wage subsidy that is granted solely on the basis of age may not be a very effective measure as opposed to a subsidy that is targeted more narrowly at the older long-term unemployment or at low-income older workers.

c. Improving the employability of older workers

Tackling weak employability among older workers requires action on three fronts: skills, job search, and better working conditions. The rewards for improved skills through training can be lower for older workers than they are for the young. It is crucial that lifelong learning policies encourage constant upgrading of skills over the working life. Public employment services may need extra resources to provide tailored help to the older unemployed. Improving occupational health and safety for workers of all ages will also assist future generations of older workers to remain in employment longer.

It is commonplace in all OECD countries to hear calls for improving training opportunities for older workers and encouraging them to avail more of such opportunities. There is indeed much to be done on this front as the incidence of training declines with age in all countries, and in some OECD countries the gap in training incidence between younger and older workers is particularly large.

One problem is that often neither employers nor older workers themselves see much advantage in investing in training to upgrade skills. From the former's perspective, there are fewer years to amortise the costs of investment in training older workers; from the latter's perspective, the opportunity cost of the time required for any investment in training is high. This suggests that an effective lifelong learning strategy would probably yield the highest returns by seeking to expand mid-career (i.e., from age 35-50) training opportunities rather than focussing heavily on workers aged 55 and over.

This is not to say that it is impossible to expand training participation among older workers. First, it is important to ensure that there are sufficient financial benefits from participating for both firms and older workers. Second, it is important to address different time horizons when devising training programmes for workers who have shorter-than-average expected working lives. This points to a need for flexible, short, or modular courses to be made available: A good example of this is the courses provided in Australia through its colleges of Technical and Further Education. For many older workers, the recognition of competences gained through working life is a motivation for participation in training: The Norwegian Competence Reform is a good example of such a practice.

With regard to active labour market programmes to help the unemployed find work, there is a clear need in many countries to devote more resources to help older job seekers. Several OECD countries have or are experimenting with targeted programmes for older workers. The U.K.'s New Deal 50 Plus is an interesting example of such an initiative though the evaluation results are rather mixed.

Several countries (e.g. Australia, Korea, Spain) have wage subsidy schemes targeted to the hiring of older unemployed workers. Again, the evaluation results for such schemes are mixed. Another possibility is to provide a wage top-up to older unemployed workers who find a new job that pays lower wages than their previous job, usually for a limited period. Such schemes exist in Germany, Japan, the U.K., and the U.S. Unfortunately, there is little rigorous evaluation of whether these schemes work for the older unemployed, and it would be highly desirable to fill this knowledge gap.

Finally, it is important to take steps to improve occupational health and safety if older workers are to carry on working, and to encourage employers to adapt working conditions to the specific needs of older workers. The Finnish VETO programme (see Box 2 above) assigns a large role to this task. Recent initiatives in Germany, France, and Belgium go in the same direction, encouraging employers and unions to invest more in promoting good age-management practices in the workplace.

3. What Should the United States Do?

While the United States is in a better situation with regard to older worker employment than many other OECD countries, there is still real scope for further reforms if it is to cope successfully with the looming challenges of an ageing workforce and prospects of slower labour force growth. Our OECD report on the United States put forward detailed recommendations for further actions under the three pillars spelt out above. In what follows, I will focus on our recommendations under two of the pillars: (i) strengthening the financial incentives to work longer; and (ii) tackling employment barriers on the side of employers.[3]

a. Rewarding work

Under this heading, we argued for the following reforms:

- Speed up the transition from 65 to 67 for the full retirement age. This will only solve part of the future financing problem, however, and additional adjustments to the parameters of Social Security will have to be considered to guarantee its sustainability. These adjustments should take account of further increases in life expectancy.

- Raise the minimum age for Social Security. Increasing the minimum age for Social Security from 62 to 64 years would both encourage later retirement and improve retirement incomes.

- Ensure disability benefits do not become an alternative route to early retirement. This would require careful monitoring of Disability Insurance claims to ensure that benefits were granted only to people with very limited opportunities in the labour market. It would be desirable more broadly to promote activation policies for Disability Insurance beneficiaries, including greater opportunities for rehabilitation.

- Limit tax advantages in private pension schemes for taking early retirement. Another complementary change would be to limit the tax advantages for those taking early retirement through private occupational systems, so that there was consistency with the proposed changes in the Social Security early-retirement age. At the same time, the eligibility age for the Earned Income Tax Credit should be extended so that it covers everyone up to the full retirement age for Social Security.

b. Tackling employment barriers on the side of employers

While there is no single measure that would dramatically increase job retention or hiring of older workers, we argued for the following reforms:

- Support further spread of defined-contribution (DC) pension schemes. From the perspective of promoting retention and hiring of older workers, DC plans have a number of advantages over defined-benefit plans: they do not encourage early retirement, and they do not raise the cost of hiring older workers relative to younger workers. Therefore, the continued spread of these plans should be supported, but it will be particularly important to ensure that there is good governance of these schemes and adequate information given to participants to help them plan their retirement.

- Eliminate the "Medicare-as-secondary-payer" rule. Currently, employers who offer health insurance to their employees aged under 65 must offer the same health insurance to employees who are eligible for Medicare. Abolishing this requirement would enhance employment opportunities for workers aged 65 and over. Of course, the budgetary consequences would need to be considered carefully, given that this proposal could involve additional public expenditures of around 3 billion dollars per year.

- Strengthen measures to combat age discrimination. Measures should be taken to strengthen the effectiveness of ADEA, especially with respect to hiring. This could include the introduction of explicit guidance in the Act concerning "disparate impact." Consideration should also be given to extending protection under the Act to people of any age rather than just to those aged 40 and over, as this could help to reduce older people being stigmatised. The exemption of smaller companies should also be reconsidered.

- Promote the business case for employing older workers. Strengthening legislation to ban age discrimination will be more effective if accompanied by campaigns to change employer attitudes. The outreach and educational activities of the Equal Employment Opportunity Commission should be expanded. Employers may also be more inclined to adopt "age-friendly" employment practices if they are given better information about the impact of labour force ageing on prospective skill shortages. Therefore, in consultation with employer groups, the government should ensure that information is collected at a national level on current and prospective skill shortages.

4. Concluding Remarks

As a result of rapid population ageing, the United States faces a risk of slower economic growth, serious labour shortages, and rising tax rates over the next few decades. By 2030, almost one-fifth of its population is projected to be aged 65 and over compared with around one-eighth in 2000. The labour force will also age and is likely to grow much more slowly than in the past. As the Baby Boom generation begins to move into retirement from 2010, or even earlier, growing expenditures on Social Security will have to be financed by taxes on a smaller number of workers relative to the number of pensioners or by cuts in the value of Social Security benefits. On the basis of current rates of labour force participation, the ratio of workers to "retirees" (i.e., all persons aged over 50 and over who are not in the labour force) is projected to decline.

But the picture is not all doom and gloom. The bottom line for the United States from the OECD review is clear: The U.S is in a relatively good position compared with most other OECD countries in terms of older workers, but there is no room for complacency. Some other OECD countries are doing better and, given the daunting challenges ahead as the population and workforce age, more needs to be done to help older Americans carry on working.

This paper has drawn on the experiences of other OECD countries and our analysis of the U.S. older worker labour market to highlight several reforms that could help achieve this objective. Among the most important are: link the retirement age to life expectancy; change employer attitudes about hiring and retaining older workers, and adapt workplace practices to the needs of a more age-diverse workforce; revamp employment programs for older job seekers; and expand training opportunities for low-skilled and mid-career workers. Actions on these fronts would certainly put the United States in a much better position to cope with the challenges posed by, and exploit the opportunities of, population ageing.

Appendix

Table A1. Reforms to national retirement income systems since 1990 in OECD countries

Country	Pension eligibility age	Adjusted retirement incentives	Change of years in benefit formula or qualifying conditions	Link to life expectancy and/or financial sustainability	Defined contribution scheme	Other
Australia	Pension age for women rising from 60 to 65. Increase from 55 to 60 in age to access private pensions.	New lump-sum bonus for deferring public pension.		Through annuity calculation in DC scheme.	Mandatory DC scheme introduced in addition to public pension.	Lower withdrawal rate for income test in the public pension.
Austria	Early retirement age increased by 1.5 years. Pension corridor between 62 and 65. Pension ages for women aligned with those of men.	Benefit reduction for early retirement introduced and set to increase. Tighter access to early retirement.	Best 15 years to 40 years.	Introduction of sustainability factor under discussion.		Reduction in accrual rate. Less generous indexation for higher pensions.
Belgium	Pension age for women aligned with that for men.	Pension bonus for workers above age 62. Different accounting for work and credit periods. Fiscal incentive to take-up private pensions only at standard pension age.	Contribution condition for early retirement at 60 tightened.			
Canada						Pre-funding of earnings-related plan.
Czech Republic	Phased increase in normal pension age to 63.	Changes in increments and reductions for early/late retirement.				
Denmark	Phased increase in normal pension age from 65 to 67.			Normal pension age linked to life expectancy.		
Finland		Increased accrual rate for people working age 63-67.	10 last years to lifetime average.	Life-expectancy multiplier (from 2010).		Basic part of national pension income-tested. Higher valorisation of past earnings and lower indexation of pensions in payment.

Country	Pension eligibility age	Adjusted retirement incentives	Change of years in benefit formula or qualifying conditions	Link to life expectancy and/or financial sustainability	Defined contribution scheme	Other
France		Changes in adjustment to benefits for early/late retirement in public and occupational pensions.	Minimum contribution period increased. Earnings measure in public scheme from best 10 to best 25 years.	Minimum contribution period to increase further with changes in life expectancy.	Targeted minimum income of 85% of minimum wage.	Lower withdrawal rate for income test in the public pension.
Germany		Reduction in benefits for retirement before 65.		Valorisation and indexation cut back as system dependency ratio worsens.	Voluntary DC pensions with tax privileges.	Phased abolition of favorable tax treatment of pension income.
Greece	Pension age rising from 58 to 65.					
Hungary	Gradual increase in pension age from 55 for women and 60 for men to 62 for both.	Accrual rates linear rather than higher for earlier years.	Pension calculation based on gross rather than net earnings.	Through annuity calculation in DC scheme.	DC scheme: mandatory for new entrants, voluntary for existing workers.	Minimum pension to be abolished. Less generous Indexation of pensions in payment. Pensions subject to income tax.
Iceland				No significant changes since 1990		
Ireland					Incentives for voluntary retirement savings.	Pre-funding of public pensions. Increase in basic pension.
Italy	Normal pension age for men increased from 60 to 65 and for women from 55 to 60. Early pension age for men with 35 years' coverage increases from 60 to 62.	Adjustment to early-retirement benefits through notional annuity calculation.	Qualification years for long-service pension increased from 37 to 40 years.	Through notional annuity calculation.		From DB to notional accounts. Less generous indexation of higher pensions.
Japan	Pension age increasing from 60 to 65.		Pensionable earnings extended to include bonuses.	Benefits adjusted to reflect expected change in dependency ratio.		Accrual rate reduced.
Korea	Pension age rising from 60 to 65.					
Luxembourg				No significant changes since 1990		
Mexico					Mandatory private DC scheme replaces public, DB plan.	

Live Longer, Work Longer: 57

Country	Pension eligibility age	Adjusted retirement incentives	Change of years in benefit formula or qualifying conditions	Link to life expectancy and/or financial sustainability	Defined contribution scheme	Other
Netherlands			Planned abolition of early retirement programme.	Shift from final to average lifetime salary in many occupational plans.		
New Zealand	Pension age increased from 60 to 65.				Voluntary DC pensions with auto-enrolment and incentives.	Pre-funding of public pension.
Norway					Mandatory employer DC contributions.	Pre-funding of public pensions.
Poland	Withdrawal of early retirement for certain groups of workers.		From best consecutive 10 in final 20 years to lifetime average.	Through notional annuity calculation in public scheme and annuity calculation in DC.	DC scheme mandatory for new entrants and workers under 30.	Abolition of basic pension. From DB to notional accounts.
Portugal	Pensionable age for women aligned with that for men at 65.	Introduction of increments for late retirement and reductions for early retirement.	From best 10 out of last 15 years to lifetime average earnings	Through notional annuity calculation.	Life-expectancy adjustment to benefits.	Less generous indexation of higher pensions.
Slovak Republic	Increase in pension ages to 62 for men and women.		From best 5 in final 10 years to lifetime average earnings.	Through annuity calculation in DC scheme.	DC scheme mandatory for new entrants and voluntary for existing workers.	From DB to points system.
Spain		Introduction of small increment for late retirement.				
Sweden			Best 15 years to lifetime average (public, earnings-related scheme).	Through calculation of notional annuity and annuity in DC schemes. Additional sustainability adjustment in notional accounts.	DC scheme mandatory for nearly all workers. Occupational plans switch from DB to DC.	From DB to notional accounts. Abolition of income-tax concessions for pensioners.
Switzerland	Pension age for women increased from 62 to 64.					Reduction in required interest rate and annuity rate in mandatory occupational plans.

Country	Pension eligibility age	Adjusted retirement incentives	Change of years in benefit formula or qualifying conditions	Link to life expectancy and/or financial sustainability	Defined contribution scheme	Other
Turkey	Pension age to increase to 65.					
United Kingdom	Women's pension age and eligibility for guarantee credit rising from 60 to 65.	Increment for deferring pension claim increased. Lump-sum option added.			Employers required to provide access to DC ("stakeholder") pension.	Increase in basic pension. Extension of means-tested supplements. Increased progressivity of earnings-related pension.
United States	Increase in full pension age from 65 to 67.	Changes in adjustment for early/late retirement.				

Source: Whiteford and Whitehouse (2006); national authorities.

Towards a Longer Worklife: Milestones of Finland and Finnish Institute of Occupational Health from 1981-2008

Professor Juhani Ilmarinen, Ph.D.

Director, Finnish Institute of Occupational Health; Professor and Director, "Life Course and Works"; and leading European authority on ageing and work issues

Introduction

The chapter introduces the long-term and sustainable efforts made in Finland to stimulate the increased utilization of older workers. The preparation for older society and for a longer and better worklife started in the early 1980s with longitudinal studies by the Finnish Institute of Occupational Health (FIOH). The first 11 years were invested in finding the facts of ageing and work followed by political efforts of ministries and national programmes for 10 years. The latest phase of sequencing can be described by the creation of new approaches, like Life Course and Work, as well as new and more focused national programmes and plans for EU-wide implementation of Good Age Management practices. The FIOH has played an important role as an expert organisation under the Ministry of Social Affairs and Health (Fingerhut et al., 2004) (Table 1).

Table 1:
Milestones of Aging and Work in Finland 1981 - 2007 (Sequencing)

1. Demographics
2. Follow-up studies (FIOH)   1981-
3. Agreement between Social Partners   1989
4. FinnAge –Research-Programm (FIOH)   1990-1996

5. Cabinet committee   1996
6. FINPAW (FIOH)   1998-2002
7. Pension Reform   2005
8. New National – Programmes   2003-2007

9. Life course and work (FIOH)   2006-
10. New Policy-Programmes   2008-
11. EU27 Implementation Programme

Research Background (1981-1996)

The demographics in the 1980s predicted that Finland would have one of the oldest workforces in the world due to the relatively large Baby Boom Generations after the turn of the 20th century. At the same time, the pension institutions raised the question: "What is the right retirement age for workers and employees?" It was seen that the options for early retirement as a solution of workforce ageing became more and more popular.

The FIOH started a follow-up study of 6,500 municipal workers and employees in 1981 and repeated the measures of the same subjects (age 44-58 years at onset) in 1985, 1992, and 1997 (Tuomi, 1997). A new concept and method of Work Ability was constructed and validated for evaluation of changes in human resources related to work during ageing (Tuomi et al., 1998).

The 4-year and 11-year follow-up of the Work Ability Index (WAI) showed some alarming results: among 30 percent of subjects the WAI decreased significantly, only in 10 percent the WAI improved, and among 60 percent it remained rather unchanged (Ilmarinen et al. 1997). The declining trend of WAI was independent of the type of work and gender. The results indicated that about one-third of the ageing workers were under the risk of losing their work ability and were potential early retirees.

The social partners were informed about the results, and they made an important mutual statement in 1989 that maintenance and promotion of work ability was their common goal. As a consequence, the FIOH planned a FinnAge Respect for the Ageing Programme for creating and testing the promotion concept of work ability in enterprises and work organisations (1990-1996) (Ilmarinen and Louhevaara, 1999). As a result of this programme, the concepts and tools for wider implementation of work ability interventions in worklife were available.

Political Activities (1996-2007)

The next phase of sequencing was based on activities of government and key ministries. A Cabinet Committee, consisting of social partners, ministries of social affairs and health, labour and education, as well as research institutions, produced 56 different recommendations in 1996 to improve the situation of older workers in the labour market. The next step was to establish a Finnish National Programme on Ageing Workers (FINPAW) with the aim to implement and realize the recommendations of the Committee. Altogether, 40 different projects, including a public information campaign, life-long learning, age- management training, and promotion of work ability beside legislative development, were carried out in 1998-2002 (Ministry of Social Affairs and Health, 2002). For example, the promotion of work ability was inserted in the Act of Occupational Health Care in 2002 and in the Act of Occupational Safety in 2003.

The largest legislative reform was the revision of the earning-related pension system, which became active in the beginning of 2005. Those benefiting from the reforms include young and old, students, and parents with small children whose pension benefits were increased. The most obvious winners are people in their 60s who stay in worklife longer. Their work contribution will add an accumulation to their pension of 4.5 percent a year from the age of 63 years to the age of 68 years (Ilmarinen, 2006). (Figure 1)

Figure 1:
Pension Reform in 2005

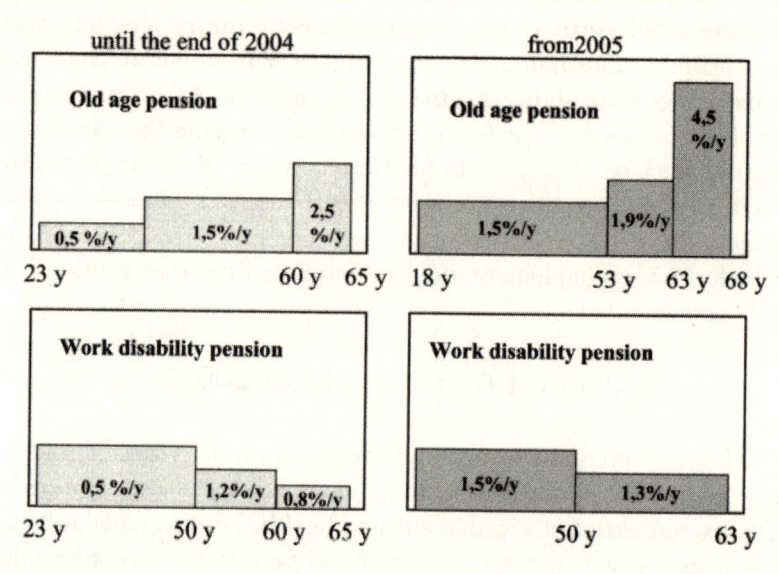

until the end of 2004

Old age pension
0,5 %/y | 1,5%/y | 2,5 %/y
23 y   60 y 65 y

from 2005

Old age pension
1,5%/y | 1,9%/y | 4,5 %/y
18 y   53 y 63 y 68 y

Work disability pension
0,5 %/y | 1,2%/y | 0,8%/y
23 y   50 y   60 y 65 y

Work disability pension
1,5%/y | 1,3%/y
50 y   63 y

    The success factors behind the FINPAW were (i) the lack of ideological controversy over the importance of ageing in the society and (ii) wide political range due to a coalition of democrats and conservatives in the government, as well as (iii) the active role of social partners, and (iv) the research institutes. The concept of "carrots first and sticks later" made the pension reform politically feasible. The carrots included the promotion of work ability of older workers and the sticks the limitations of early retirement options. Altogether, the groundwork for a flexible pension reform started in 1989, and it took more than 15 years before it was accepted.

    New national programmes were also introduced directly after the FINPAW; they included:

- Coping at Work 2000-2003 (Ministry of Labour)
- TYKES: Finnish Workplace Development Programme, 2004-2009 (Ministry of Labour)
- VETO: programme promoting the attractiveness of worklife 2003-2007 (Ministry of Social Affairs and Health)
- KESTO: programme for sustainable work career development 2004-2007 (FIOH)
- NOSTE: programme for increasing the competency of working adults 2003-2007 (Ministry of Education)

The concept of national programmes is characteristic for Finland. They are believed to be more effective than a large set of single projects of academic institutions without national coordination. Also, the financing of the research activities with public money generates possibilities to focus on sustainable ways to utilize ideas and workers. This approach is feasible for a small and rather homogenous country like Finland, but it could also work as a regional approach for countries with a much larger and diverse population.

Employment Rates of Older Workers

Based on the long-term active ageing policy, the employment rates have been improved in Finland better than in the reference countries of the European Union. The improvement of employment rates of the 55-64-year-old population between 1997 and 2006 was 18.9 percent in Finland, and the employment level reached 54.5 percent in 2006. After Sweden, Denmark, and the United Kingdom, Finland had the 4th highest employment rate of older workers in the European Union in 2006. In the second place of improvements in employment rates was the Netherlands with 15.7 percent from 1997 to 2006. The employment rates of 60-67-year-olds from 2003 to 2006 in Finland are shown in Figure 2.

Figure 2:
Employment Rates of 60-67 year-olds from 2003-2006 in Finland

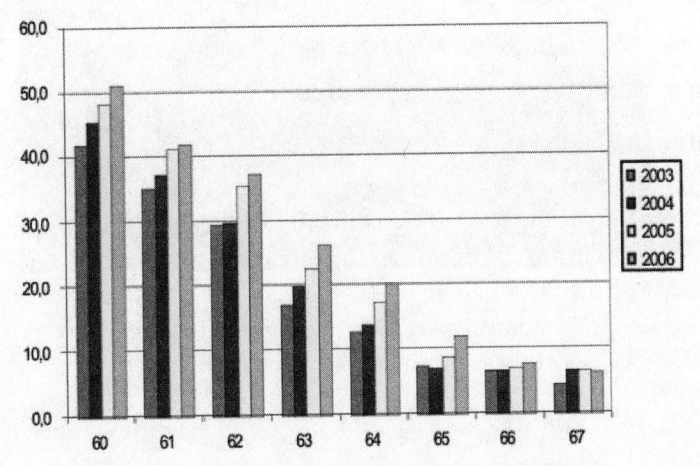

Source: Center of Statistics, Finland

The international comparison of employment rates of older workers shows, however, that the European Union is on average far behind the best countries in the world. The highest employment rates of 55-64-year-olds are shown in Iceland, followed by Norway, Switzerland, Japan, and the U.S. (Figure 3). The average figure of the European Union is almost 20 percent lower and rather independent of the different grouping of the European Union member states. This means that the input and output as a competitive factor of older workers from Europe is less utilized than in the best countries. The difference is even larger when the comparison is made according to the employment rates of the older female population. The average employment rates of 55-64-year-old women in the European Union are about 33 percent. Therefore, the older female population serves as the largest workforce potential in the European Union. A crucial question is how older women can be motivated and become an attractive work force in the European Union.

Figure 3:
Employment Rates of 55-64 year-olds in Selected Countries Compared with Average Figures of the European Union in 2005

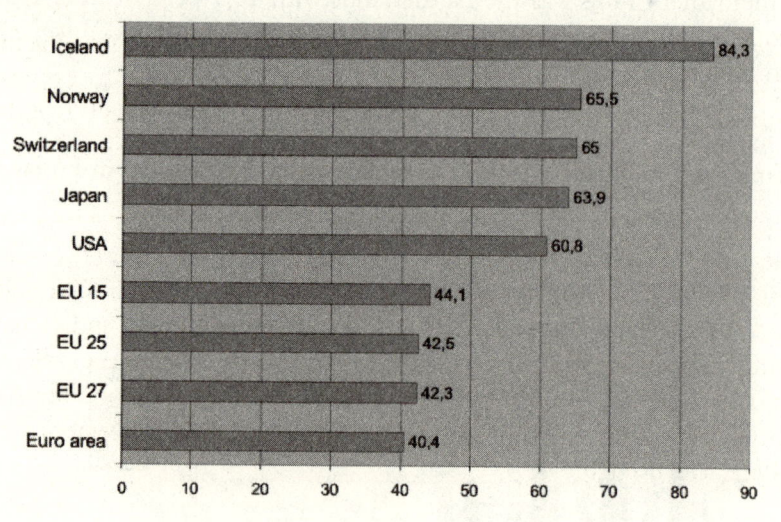

Country	Employment Rate
Iceland	84,3
Norway	65,5
Switzerland	65
Japan	63,9
USA	60,8
EU 15	44,1
EU 25	42,5
EU 27	42,3
Euro area	40,4

Concepts and Solutions for Older Workers in Work Organisations

During the last decade, several validated concepts have been implemented successfully in the enterprises and work organisations: (i) Age Management, (ii) Employability, (iii) Work Ability and Work Ability Index, (iv) Promotion of Work Ability (PWA), and (v) Age Management Coaching.

In the following, short descriptions of the tools will be given.

Age Management

Age Management is a concept emphasizing three levels of action needed for the challenges of ageing: The roles of individuals, enterprises, and society are all important. The problems of individuals and enterprises related to ageing are closely connected. When older workers worry over health problems, the companies worry about the costs of sick leaves. When older workers are unsure about their ability to learn new skills, the enterprises are afraid of the lack of key competencies and of investments in life-long learning. Society tries to prevent the early retirement and work disability costs. Ageing creates problems at all levels, but the age management concept also provides solutions for each level. Individuals can adopt healthy lifestyles, companies can invest in health promotion programmes, and society can support health promotion by preventive policies. The targets of the actions can be set, too: better functional capacities and health for the individuals, less sick-leave costs for the enterprises, and later retirement as a goal for the society. However, before the results at the society level can be seen, the targets of the individuals and enterprises should be achieved first. Therefore, the role of individuals and enterprises are crucial–public policies alone are not effective enough. The three levels of Age Management are illustrated in Figure 4.

Figure 4:
Three Levels of Age Management

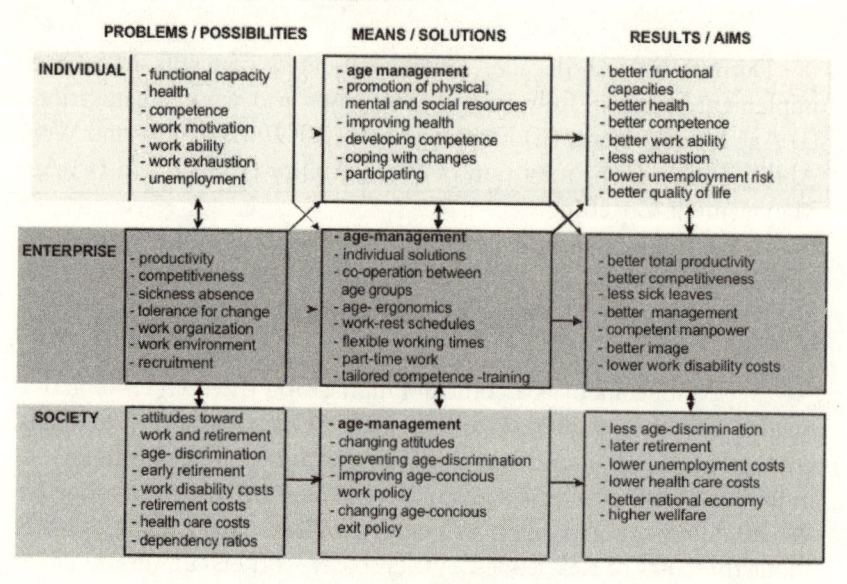

	PROBLEMS / POSSIBILITIES	MEANS / SOLUTIONS	RESULTS / AIMS
INDIVIDUAL	- functional capacity - health - competence - work motivation - work ability - work exhaustion - unemployment	- age management - promotion of physical, mental and social resources - improving health - developing competence - coping with changes - participating	- better functional capacities - better health - better competence - better work ability - less exhaustion - lower unemployment risk - better quality of life
ENTERPRISE	- productivity - competitiveness - sickness absence - tolerance for change - work organization - work environment - recruitment	- age-management - individual solutions - co-operation between age groups - age- ergonomics - work-rest schedules - flexible working times - part-time work - tailored competence -training	- better total productivity - better competitiveness - less sick leaves - better management - competent manpower - better image - lower work disability costs
SOCIETY	- attitudes toward work and retirement - age- discrimination - early retirement - work disability costs - retirement costs - health care costs - dependency ratios	- age-management - changing attitudes - preventing age-discrimination - improving age-concious work policy - changing age-concious exit policy	- less age-discrimination - later retirement - lower unemployment costs - lower health care costs - better national economy - higher welfare

Employability

Employability has several definitions, but the special feature of the Finnish definition is that it takes the role of work ability into consideration along with employment, education, health, and social policies. Integration of the work ability concept in enterprises and public policies will improve the employment rates, as well as the human and economic well-being.

Work Ability

The new approach is the Work Ability, the relation between work and human resources. The work includes environmental, contextual, and organisational features. The human resources covers the health and functional capacities, and the competence as well as values and attitudes of the individual. These core dimensions of work ability should be in balance with each other (Ilmarinen and Tuomi, 2004; Ilmarinen et al., 2005). Recent studies have added the close-environment outside worklife into other dimensions, such as family and economic matters. The work ability concept stresses the roles of employers and employees. The supervisors have the authority in the fourth floor of the work ability house-model (Figure 5). The organisation of work in productive ways is their primary task. The individuals are more responsible for their health and competence matters. However, neither the supervisors nor the older workers-employee alone can reach a good work ability–they can only do it together.

Figure 5:
The Core Dimensions of Work Ability

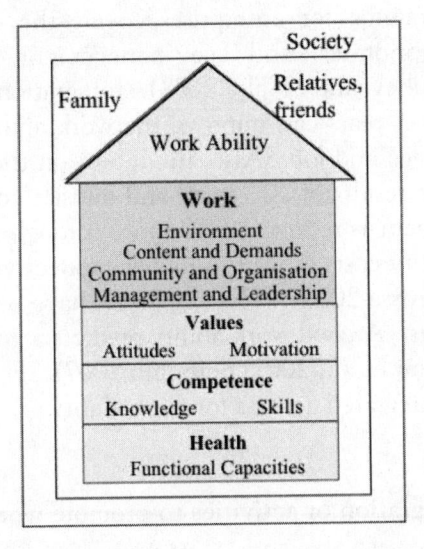

```
                          Society
              Family         Relatives,
                             friends
                   Work Ability

              Work
              Environment
              Content and Demands
              Community and Organisation
              Management and Leadership
              Values
              Attitudes      Motivation
              Competence
              Knowledge      Skills
              Health
              Functional Capacities
```

The work ability can be evaluated by the Work Ability Index (WAI) developed by FIOH researchers (Tuomi et al., 1998). The WAI questionnaire consists of seven validated items, and the predictive power of the instrument with regard to staying at work or being granted a work disability pension in 11 years is high. The WAI introduces the current status of work ability and classifies the risks in four levels. The recent representative survey of work ability showed that the average work ability decline is linear with age. This means that the balance between work and human resources is declining during ageing. It has been calculated that the cost of work ability decline of age groups over 45 years is about 800 million euros per year in Finland. Therefore, the promotion of work ability is urgently needed.

Promotion of Work Ability

The promotion of work ability (PWA) covers both the actions needed at work and in human resources (Ilmarinen, 1999). The experiences in enterprises during the last decade have shown that it is seldom only one action that is needed for the promotion. In most cases, at least three promoting actions are needed, which can be identified by additional surveys, along with the WAI (Costa et al., 2005). A typical programme for enterprises covers the corporate health promotion, ergonomics, and age management training of the supervisors (Louhevaara et al., 2003). Integration of these three activities over 1-3 years can improve the work ability of employees, independent of age and job. Also, the return on the investment has been good: The results of 200 small and midsize companies showed that the investment is returned 3-10 times through lower sick leaves and work disability costs as well as higher productivity (Näsman and Ahonen, 1999; Rissa 2007). The employers have been satisfied with their investments. A good work ability predicts a good well-being in retirement (Tuomi et al., 2001; Seitsamo 2007). Figure 6 shows the importance of integrated actions for work ability.

Figure 6:
The role of integration of activities to promote work ability

(modified by Dr. Richenhagen)

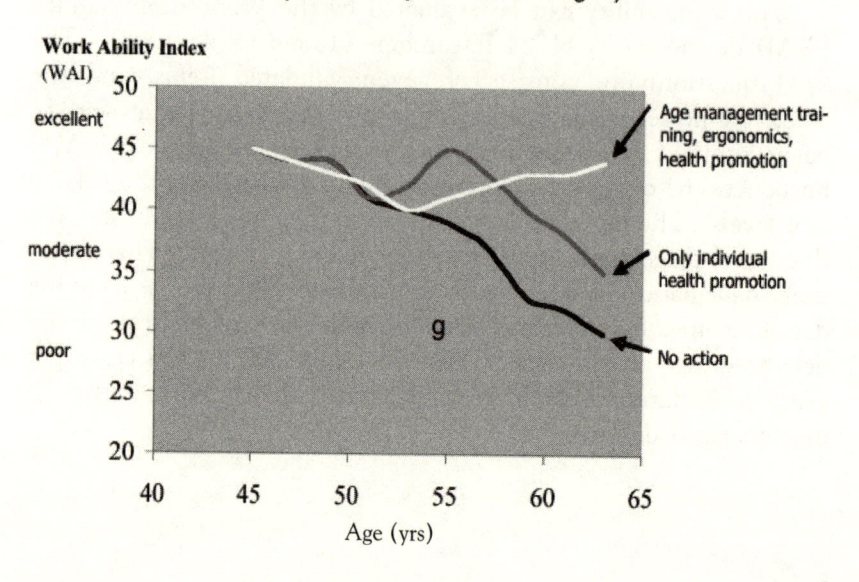

Age Management Coaching

Age Management Coaching for enterprises includes the learning of concepts and training tools for work ability promotion. The FIOH is developing a three-day international training programme in Age Management. The programme consists of analysis of globalisation, new technology, demography and their consequences; and of challenges for individuals, enterprises, and society. The target of the training is to improve the awareness level in age-related matters, change the attitudes towards ageing, and enhance the possibilities to create solutions in the enterprises and work organisations. The training will be focused on managers and supervisors as well as on employees. After the pilot programme in different worklife settings in 2008, the handbook of Age Management Coaching Programme for coaches and workbook for attendants will be published by FIOH in 2009.

Life Course and Work for Longer Work Careers

The newest development of FIOH is the Life Course and Work approach. A proactive approach for better and longer work careers should cover all generations in worklife. Therefore, FIOH started a new Life Course and Work Theme in 2006 aimed at developing innovative solutions and tools for young, middle-aged, and older generations at work. The toolbox under development looks like the following:

- Towards working life (school)
- From school to work (vocational school)
- Back to working life (unemployed people)
- Successful Senior (40+)
- Physical work and age
- Age Management Coaching Programme
- Occupational Health Services for Age-Integrated Working Life
- Healthy and Productive Working Hours
- Management of Life Course Transitions

The key products of the Life Course and Work Theme in 2006-2010 will be the Successful Senior–Group method for empowerment of 40+ employees, and the Age Management Coaching Programme for supervisors and employees, as mentioned earlier. The products for schools are already in the dissemination and implementation phase in Finland.

Implementation of Good Age Management Practices in the European Union

According to the Lisbon target, the employment rate of the age 55-64 population should be at least 50 percent by 2010 in the European Union. Today, the distance to the target is on average about 8 percent. The current European Union strategies are not necessarily powerful enough to reach the target. Therefore, the Good Corporate Age Management Practices should be urgently implemented in the European Union. The Finnish concepts and practices have shown that the employment rates of older workers can be improved significantly. Also, during the last decade many projects and programmes in age management in several countries have been carried out (Reday-Mulvey, 2005). In the European Union, the Best Practices in Age Management was published recently (Taylor, 2006; Naegele and Walker, 2006). The report includes almost 130 successful company cases in European Union Member States. This means that the knowledge and experience level is high enough for broader implementation of age management practices.

A general idea could be the Smart Region approach. First, in each country 1-3 Smart Regions should be identified. Smart Region means that the social partners (employer associations and trade unions) are ready for co-operation, the infrastructures (e.g., health and education services) have competent service providers, and the different actors at the corporate level (managers and employees) consider the implementation necessary and important.

The next phase is to "train the trainers": The key actors needed in the Region will be trained for age management, and their task will be to tailor the information to local conditions and disseminate it. The age management training includes two core elements: The Age Management Coaching Programme from FIOH and the Good Corporate Age Management Practices from the European Union. The preliminary plan will be worked out next and introduced for comments from the key organisations in the European Union later in 2008.

We at FIOH believe that these initiatives can have multiple benefits: provide employers with older workers who have the skills and abilities to meet their workforce needs, enable older workers to continue in productive activities for longer periods of time for their personal and financial benefit, allow countries to increase the sustainability of their social programmes in times when people have greater longevity, and have a positive impact on the entire society because older workers can continue in productive activities and have a better quality of life.

The New Retirement: Myths and Models

Helen Dennis, M.A.

Nationally recognized leader on issues of aging, employment, and retirement; author, weekly columnist, speaker, and consultant

Terminology is Antiquated

Society is having increasing difficulty with the term "retirement." For some, the term just doesn't conform with reality; for others, it has a negative meaning, which may emanate, in part, from the nature of its root word.

"Retirement" comes from the French word "retirer," meaning "to withdraw." The term "tirer" also refers to drawing out or enduring, which is related to the French word "martir," in English, martyr.[1] The definition of a martyr is one who is tortured and voluntarily dies for something of great value. Clearly on an etymological basis, "retirement" does not have a positive connotation.

Those who object to the term retirement have their reasons. Retirement has been referred to as an outdated form of social engineering, a concept that isn't a natural part of the human life cycle.[2] Others suggest it is a word that means too many things to too many people. "It is no longer as simple as working most of one's life, retiring and then sitting in a rocking chair or playing golf."[3] Lydia Bronte, in her book entitled *The Longevity Factor*,[4] states that the old concept of retirement as the American dream is gone. Retirement as a period of leisure at the end of adult life has become a blurred dream. For example, the "traditional retirement" that equates retirement exclusively with leisure is based on false assumptions such as: people don't like their work, cognitive skills and the ability to perform inevitably decline with age, and older people always find leisure more satisfying than work. These erroneous assumptions, associated with an industrial society and a previous century in which longevity increased by almost 30 years from beginning to end, lead to an unrealistic view of retirement in today's world.

Others argue that the word "retirement" is the problem. What is needed is a word that conveys continuous participation, not withdrawal, at least for the many who want to remain actively involved. When students complete four years of college, they listen to a commencement address upon graduation.[5] Perhaps we should look at the period following retirement as a time of re-commencement; older workers are graduating from their regular career jobs, in many cases with the intent of continuing to add value on a part-time or full-time basis.

The French solved the terminology problem by using different words. They refer to retirement as *La Troisième Age*, or The Third Age. This period of life is viewed as a time to give back to society and to share one's experiences and resources with others, a time for reflection rather than retreat. Elders are seen as a living bridge between yesterday and today.[6] In the U.S., Fordham University formally adopted this concept by naming their department on aging The Third Age Center.

AARP has become sensitive to the word retirement. It changed its name from the American Association of Retired Persons to AARP, purposely omitting the word retirement. This change is in response to the 17 million AARP members who are working and to the many Baby Boomers who do not identify with traditional retirement. The Boomers are a highly sought-after group, representing the AARP membership of today and tomorrow. To retain their existing Boomer memberships and to woo the new ones, AARP has made several strategic changes. The name change was a major one, appealing to this 78 million cohort who typically are not joiners[7] and who intend to age in ways that are very different from their parents.

New words are emerging. For example, "Renewment™" was created by a group of Southern California mid-life career women who are part of Project Renewment, a grass roots movement of women creating a new kind of future for themselves. They felt "retirement" did not convey their vision and approach to the next 30 years. A future of vitality, passion, meaning, and opportunity was better conveyed through a new term.

Authors Jeri Sedlar and Rick Miner reject the term and meaning of retirement in their book entitled, *"Don't Retire, Rewire."*[9] Ken Dychtwald and co-authors in a Harvard Business Review article write, "It's time to retire retirement."[10] Their advice is directed to employers who will face skills shortages and need the talents and capabilities of their retirement-eligible employees.

Expectations are High

Adults have high expectations regarding their own retirement. In a series of interviews of 1,000 people over age 42, both working and retired, researchers confirmed that many individuals expect to live much longer lives. Almost 80 percent believed they would likely live to at least 75 years. About 40 percent of those working felt that it is at least somewhat likely they would live to 85, and approximately 25 percent believed that they would live to be 90.[11] Additionally, working people wanted to have the same opportunity for early retirement as the current generations of retirees, even though they are destined to live significantly longer.[12]

Pre-retirees also expect quality from their retirement years. In my work with more than 10,000 employees preparing for their future, no one ever stated that he or she wanted less income, less fulfillment, or less fun in later life. In fact, most people expect an even better life than they are currently experiencing. They want less stress, increased freedom, and more choices.[13]

Retirement as a Dynamic Journey, Not a Destination

Retirement as a destination suggests that there is just one stop, and you know when you are there. More realistically, retirement is a journey. Robert Atchley, the noted sociologist, delineated this journey as a process.[14] He explained various phases of retirement: the honeymoon phase, the disenchantment phase, the orientation phase, and the stability phase. Briefly, the honeymoon phase is when the retiree is thrilled with the retirement experience, is busy, excited, and very happy. In the disenchantment phase, individuals experience a let-down, often following unexpected financial and health problems. The orientation phase occurs when an individual reviews how decisions are made and the choices available, and makes the necessary adjustments. Finally, the stability phase suggests a consistency in one's life. It does not mean a period of no change. Rather it suggests there is clarity in how one wants to lead his or her life and how those decisions are made. The key point in Atchley's description of this process is that retirement is a dynamic period of life and older adults can move back and forth between phases.

The Working Retired

A new group is emerging—the working retired. In this era, one cannot fully discuss retirement without considering continued employment. Studies consistently confirm that a substantial majority of mid-life adults and older are available and intend to work during their retirement years.

For example, a study recently conducted for AARP found that 80 percent of Baby Boomers plan to continue working in retirement. More than 30 percent expect to work part-time, mainly for the interest or enjoyment of work, while approximately 25 percent expect to work part-time for the income.[15]

A logical question is who will hire the millions of mid-life adults who are reported to be ready, willing, and able to work? With the documented and projected talent shortages,[16] some companies are developing innovative policies and practices to retain "senior stars."[17] Deloitte Consulting launched a Senior Leaders program that encouraged high-talent executives to redesign their jobs instead of taking early retirement. Chevron is developing programs to retain key managers for a longer time. Monsanto and Prudential are using retirees as temporary workers in jobs that involve everything from answering telephones to sophisticated technical work. GE Information Services hires retired engineers to service older technical systems that are still in use. Group Health offers opportunities to nurses five years from retirement to mentor, teach, and work part-time thereafter. Weyerhaeuser implemented a delayed retirement program offering a 25-hour workweek while retaining health benefits.

Mature workers have increased resources to find job opportunities. Among them are websites that specialize in jobs for older workers,[18] and search firms that specialize in filling executive positions with workers 55 and older on a full-time or part-time basis.

Although there is a growing need for talent, mid-life and older adults still face obstacles to employment. The first obstacle for mature workers is job fit. They must have the required professional and personal qualifications to fit with particular positions. Computer literacy is frequently a requirement, not an option.

The second obstacle is age discrimination, which continues to be an issue even though the Age Discrimination in Employment Act protects workers 40 and older against age-based decisions in employment, termination, promotion, and training. Although age discrimination is illegal, it persists. Mid-life adults seeking jobs are highly aware of this and often ask, "Will anyone hire me at my age?" Many become discouraged and stop looking after a period of time.

The prevalence of age discrimination in employment was documented in a study that paired a 32-year old with a 57-year old, provided them with the same resume and work qualifications, and sent them to have employment interviews.[19] It was found that the older job seeker was perceived to be the subject of age discrimination 40 percent of the time. This rate is higher than that of a race discrimination study conducted by the same researchers, using the same methodology, in which race discrimination occurred 20 to 25 percent of the time. Although discrimination is unacceptable under any conditions, this study pointed out that it is more prevalent than expected.

Movements and Organizations

The new retirement has spawned new movements and organizations:

The Life Planning Network (LPN):[20] This community of diverse professionals provides a broad spectrum of life planning services and resources for the third age, a period of time that represents new possibilities for living with fulfillment and purpose. LPN offers professional development, support, and opportunity to create and shape the field of Third Age Life Planning, advancing the cause of self and social renewal.

WomanSage:[21] WomanSage is a national non-profit, membership organization dedicated to educating, empowering, and fostering mentoring relationships among women at midlife. It focuses on financial literacy, women's health, the self, inner and outer beauty, careers and transitions, caregiving, and relationships. A news-based website, annual conferences, monthly salon meetings, and a network of special interest groups are benefits to their members.

The Transition Network (TNTN):[22] The Transition Network provides a national community for women over 50 as they move from their career to whatever is next and helps them discover new opportunities, perspectives, and ways to make an impact. The programs are designed to sustain their sense of accomplishment and to help them find intellectual stimulation, have fun, and make a positive impact on the wider community. TTN offers educational programs, advocacy, special interest groups, and volunteer opportunities.

Project Renewment™[23] : Project Renewment is a grassroots movement of career women 55 and older who meet in small groups to explore issues and concerns related to retirement and post-career living. (Forming a group is described in the book *Project Renewment: The First Retirement Model for Career Women* by Bernice Bratter and Helen Dennis.[24]) It also fosters an independent process that suggests how to intentionally design a future that is equal to or more gratifying than previous working years.

Myths of the Old Models

Preparing for the future is not a new concept. Retirement preparation programs date back to the 1950s. However, the models from five, ten, or twenty years ago do not reflect the complexity and diversity of the new retirement. The following seven myths describe defunct models that, if used exclusively, will limit individuals in creating a secure and fulfilling third chapter of life.

Myth #1: Finances is the only important topic.

Financial planning is imperative but not sufficient in planning for the future. Evaluating one's financial assets, projected income, and financial needs is key to developing an effective financial retirement plan. However, one can have a superb financial plan and still experience a miserable retirement. Key issues regarding what to do, where to live, how to maintain health and vitality, and how to build relationships are important partners to financial planning.

Myth #2: Paternalism is appropriate.

Corporate paternalism essentially is history. Over the past 10 years, the move towards increased self-reliance has occurred both within the workplace and in retirement as employees have become increasingly responsible for their benefits choices, pension contributions, and health plans, as well as for their own skills.[25][26][27] Therefore, programs and services that prepare individuals for retirement must provide the tools that will enable them to become good managers for themselves and their families.

Myth #3: Retirement planning should have a male focus.

It is impossible to ignore one-half of the labor force that also plans to retire–namely women. Although men and women do share core retirement concerns, there are issues that are female issues. For example, women have different attitudes towards financial planning and are less likely than men to be very confident in their financial planning for retirement, their ability to cover basic expenses, and their ability to support themselves in retirement.[28] Furthermore, many women retire alone and staying socially connected is a topic of concern to them.[29] Although books have been written on retirement planning for women, only a few address the non-financial issues.

Myth #4: Retirement planning is for "me" only.

Retirement affects more than just the retiree; it is a family affair. Spouses are an integral part of the planning process and should be active participants. In planning for the future, it is important to consider the possible surprises and opportunities in mid-to later-life, such as caring for aging parents, the return of adult children, and even raising grandchildren. The family is a dynamic institution, often requiring care, attention, and resources from a generation planning for its next life chapter.

Myth #5: Every couple is heterosexual.

This is clearly false and is rarely, if ever, acknowledged in retirement planning. Gay and lesbian couples are aging, planning for their future, and retiring. Their retirement planning needs may or may not be different from those of heterosexual couples. However, what is important is to include these couples within the mainstream in retirement education services.

Myth #6: I can only learn in a classroom.

Online learning is the wave of the present and future. Increasingly, large companies are offering more online educational opportunities for their employees. Corporations are spending $66 billion a year on training. Twenty percent is spent on e-learning and 80 percent on traditional classroom instruction. These figures are expected to change to 40 percent for online learning and 60 percent for traditional classroom learning.[30] It is very likely that companies will increasingly provide retirement education online.[31] Additionally, individuals can have free access to a vast amount of information on the Internet, although selecting the most relevant, reliable, and valid information can be a challenge. On May 14, 2008, Google listed 7,040,000 web pages under retirement planning; 276,000 web pages were listed for early retirement planning and 292,000 web pages for pre-retirement planning.

Myth #7: Retirement planners are exclusively financial specialists.

Financial planners providing retirement services are expanding their focus. They are beginning to include non-financial issues such as transitions, housing, and lifestyles, taking a broader approach to retirement. An example is SecurePath by Transamerica.

Additionally, retirement planners are emerging from the field of life coaching. At a 2007 National Conference on Positive Aging, the Life Planning Network sponsored a pre-conference on the third age. Of the 150 attending, over three-quarters identified themselves as life coaches in their roles as social workers, psychologists, and licensed clinical therapists. Their company titles indicate a more holistic approach to the traditional retirement planning. Examples include: Third Age Life Crafting, Encore Life Planning, Opus II, New Directions, Innovations: Creating New Visions for Retirement, Life Spring Coaching, Transition Counseling Solutions, Life Clarity Coaching, and Pathmaking for Life.[32]

Enhancements for Retirement Planning: New Models

One approach to developing new and relevant models of retirement planning is to avoid the term retirement and its traditional meaning of leisure and rest. The following is an attempt to describe components for new models that are meaningful for today's adults. The one prerequisite to each of the suggested components is financial education and planning.

Life management planning

This conveys a much broader approach because it encompasses but is not limited to retirement planning. It begins the first day at work and continues throughout a lifetime. Ideally, such a program would be provided on a continuum of topics by all employers so that when an employee leaves one company and goes to another, he or she would continue enhancing life-management planning skills with the new employer. This includes subjects such as income, savings, investment, and spending patterns; work-family issues such as maternity and paternity leave, child care, and eldercare; stress management and achieving a balance in life; and a range of retirement issues such as geographic location.

Rehirement planning

This type of program is designed specifically for those considering to work longer. Some questions it addresses are: Do I want to work for continued income, the social contacts, the satisfaction and self-esteem of continuing to add value, or some combination thereof? Do I want structure that the workplace provides, or do I want to be self-employed? Do I have the skills to contribute productively, or do I need further training and education? Does my spouse/partner/family understand why I want to work, and do I have the job-seeking skills to get the job I want?

Health and wealth planning

Surveys confirm that the two greatest concerns expressed by mid-life workers center on finances and health. Here is an opportunity to blend the two. Individuals need to understand personal finances; the relationship between finances and various kinds of insurance, including health and long-term care; and how to maintain health and vitality in the normal aging process. Interventions such as exercise, nutrition, staying intellectually engaged, avoiding risk factors for disease and disability, and developing a health/wealth plan will help individuals to age successfully.

A different life

This concept is appropriate for individuals who seek to make major changes in their next chapter of life. Such a program helps the individual with self-evaluation, obtaining relevant information, communicating with a spouse or partner, taking risks, and embracing change.

Such major changes might involve relocation to another part of the U.S. or to a foreign country; divorce, marriage, or remarriage; living in a houseboat or a motor home; entering a degree program or continuing with education; pursuing a different career or starting a business; and involvement in volunteer activities or political activism.

Gains from change

Charles Handy, the British social philosopher, discusses change in his book, *The Age of Unreason*.[33] He makes several assumptions about change that are applicable to the new retirement and its impact on the individual.

Assumption #1: The changes in this decade are different, not part of a pattern, and are confusing.

Commentary: The new retirement is revolutionary. For the first time in history, some people are likely to retire for as long as they worked in their primary career; some people may never retire, while others will work into older age. Increased life expectancy and the blending of work, education, and leisure will make the last third of life as dynamic as any previous life stages, challenging the conventional meaning of retirement.

Assumption #2: Little changes can make the biggest difference in our lives.

Commentary: A small positive change in health behaviors can influence the quality of one's retirement as well as the longevity. Small and consistent savings can affect income security. A decision on health insurance can avert possible health crises.

Assumption #3: Upside-down thinking may be necessary for the new changes.

Commentary: Working in retirement is not illogical. Getting an advanced degree in later life is not outrageous. Doing what you've never done before in later life is an opportunity worth pursuing. Running a marathon at 75 is a reasonable goal, not an absurdity.

To ensure a successful third chapter of life, many individuals may need to change or modify their behaviors in response to increased life expectancy, more dynamic environments, and personal expectations. Retirement professionals should provide the tools for individuals to adapt to this period of time in ways that are valuable, relevant, and engaging. New concepts, language, and methods are required to make a "successful third chapter" within the reach of all Americans. It is not only a worthy goal, it is achievable.

The Role of Enabling Institutions in Tapping the Potential of an Aging America

Scott A. Bass, Ph.D.

Provost and Chief Academic Officer, American University, Washington, DC

There is a growing literature indicating that the Baby Boom generation intends to live their later years in a manner differently than the previous generation (Bass, 1995; Freedman, 2007; Moody, 1988; Morrow-Howell, Hinterlong & Sherraden, 2001; Rowe & Kahn, 1998; Zinke & Tattershall, 2000). For the most part this literature indicates restlessness with the notion of retirement as a time of disengagement from the social and economic fabric of society. Further, rather than just stating what Baby Boomers don't want– retirement as we know it–there are findings that reveal a desire for meaningful engagement not unlike that search which has been evident throughout the Baby Boomer life course. Yet, it is not clear how this aging cohort will be able to accomplish these desires with the current opportunities available.

While there is evidence that the pattern which has existed over the past 50 years of retirement occurring at earlier ages has abated, the exact pattern of retirement activity among Baby Boomers has yet to unfold. Nevertheless, the trend since 1985 has been toward older adults continuing to work. The vast majority of those aged 65 and older, about 84 percent, have exited the workforce; however, a small but growing number remain. This is most prevalent for those who are closest to the traditional retirement age, with nearly 30 percent of those 65-69 years of age still engaged in the labor force (U.S. Bureau of Labor Statistics, 2007), up from less than 19 percent in 1985 (U.S. Bureau of Labor Statistics, 2004). According to surveys, many Baby Boomers indicate that they intend to continue working past the traditional retirement age of 65. In fact, a widely quoted AARP survey in 2003 revealed that nearly 70 percent of the Baby Boom population report that they expect to continue working in their retirement years (AARP, 2003). With a lifetime history of preventive health, better educational preparation, and a higher standard of living with fewer occupational hazards than previous generations, this cohort of future older individuals is better positioned to make this expressed interest of working later in life a reality.

AARP noted the changing retirement trends and behavior of older Americans:

> Many spend their time relaxing or traveling if they can—but very few hold down a full-time job or continue their careers. Younger retirees and baby boomers, on the other hand, are looking for something very different. Both these groups view retirement as a transition of lifestyles rather than the abrupt end of a job, a new opportunity rather than the conclusion of a career. Nor do they necessarily view any particular age as the end of an active life, including work. (AARP, 2005, p.11).

Nevertheless, reality has a powerful influence over desire–and the preferences of Baby Boomers are about to meet these realities. Members of the Baby Boom generation, those born between 1946 and 1964, will turn 65 between the years 2011-2029. It is important to consider the great diversity among groups of older people, including the aging Baby Boom generation, when attempting to forecast their future. Although better educated and healthier than previous cohorts, there remain many among this generation who have not had the advantages of college and advanced study. A range of financial circumstances, health conditions, attitudes toward work, and family situations characterize this generation not unlike any other. Some are poor, some are financially overextended, and some are disabled and cannot work.

Still, there are those Baby Boomers who will age productively–and by sheer numbers there will be more in this generation to achieve this status than ever before. They will be in relatively good health, they will continue to be mentally and physically active, and, as stated earlier, a subset of this group will be looking for an experience as they grow older that is different than what they witnessed for their parents.

As individuals age, they accumulate and aggregate life experiences. For those who have had a life of hardship, these experiences compound over time. Paralleling these disadvantaged survivors are those who have lived a life of well being; they too will accumulate assets that will provide advantages in later life (Dannefer, 2003). This chapter is intended to explore this subset of the Baby Boom generation, those healthy and able, who have options and resources. They are the product of a life that has provided a cumulative advantage and, as they approach traditional retirement age, are able to weigh options and create a new path in later life or to continue on the path well traveled.

As indicated earlier, the work participation of older individuals reveals some modest growth over historical trends; however, the eventual exiting of a significant portion of the 78 million Baby Boomers from work will have a variety of implications for different industries and regions of the country. As early as 1997 the Hudson Institute began to forecast labor shortages in selected industries as a result of the projected retirement of the Baby Boom generation (Judy & D'Amico, 1997). Shortages are anticipated in selected industries and occupations that are dependent upon a highly educated and experienced workforce. Further, some federal and state agencies/ departments have been subjected to episodic hiring freezes that have distorted their age profile, some with large numbers of Baby Boomers facing retirement and too few in line to replace them. Other shortages have surfaced in regional markets of the health care industry among nurses and physicians, as well as among public school teachers– particularly among instructors of science and mathematics. According to the Hudson Institute, as we look forward to the immediate future, demand for selected specialists will provide incentives to recruit and retain older workers.

So we have the perfect storm brewing...large numbers of Americans entering the traditional twilight of their working careers, interest among many to reinvent retirement as we know it, and potential talent shortages in selected labor markets. These shortages of specialized scientists, health professionals, engineers, and others can result in declines in productivity and in the nation's economic growth.

Japan, a society whose aging has advanced faster than the United States with 20 percent of the population over age 65, has been particularly concerned about the impact of an aging population on its economy. As Japanese scholar John Creighton Campbell writes:

Efforts to help older people work are the most unusual aspect of Japan's policy toward the elderly. Most European countries have been trying to move aging workers out of the labor force to help solve their problems of youth unemployment. The United States has concentrated on removing legal barriers to older people retaining their jobs, as through the Age Discrimination in Employment Act, but has done relatively little to improve the ability of the elderly to work, or encourage employers to hire or keep them. Only Japan pursues a consistently positive policy to job maintenance and creation for older people, and has put employment policy near the top of the government's measures to deal with the aging society (Campbell, 1992, p.254).

Historically, old age policy within the United States has been driven primarily by health and human service advocates concerned about the welfare of an aging population in need of economic and social supports. If older people are considered by policy makers as a problem in need of remediation, a very different set of policies emerge than if they are viewed as a national economic resource in search of opportunity. More recently, Japan has balanced its economic development perspective for older people with a set of health and welfare programs. Alternatively, the United States has yet to provide this balance of new initiatives for work alternatives to its array of social programs for older people.

The United States and the other industrialized countries have much to learn from Japan in developing policies and programs that seek to involve older people in meaningful work after retirement from lifetime careers. There are, however, trends toward utilizing older workers to a substantially greater degree, stimulated by several driving forces: the increase in longevity of 30 years during the last century, with age no longer a determinant of ability to add value; the shift from an industrial to a knowledge-based working world, with emphasis on brains rather than brawn; the reality that there will be a smaller number of younger workers; and a heightened concern about the unsustainability of social programs.

The Advantaged

For those approaching age 60 and beyond who are active and enjoy their work, many may continue to work beyond age 65 and well into their 70s. Role models abound with older policy makers, college presidents, elected officials, and corporate leaders continuing on a fast track well beyond age 70. For these individuals, chronological age has a lesser hold on their engagement in work. The work they are doing is fulfilling, engaging, challenging, and rewarding. They seek to continue participating in what they enjoy, find meaningful, and where they feel needed.

While this may be a modest percentage of the Baby Boom population, it still represents millions of individuals who will have the capacity and interest to continue working past age 65. Surveys have indicated that even among the recently retired, large numbers would like to return to part-time work if they could (Barth, McNaught, and Rizzi, 1995).

Table 1 below provides a summary of the range of flexible workplace options potentially available to those who are interested. While a number of different options are possible, there is a limited array of actual options available that meet all of the personal rewards Baby Boomers are seeking in later life. Many of the most desired options that provide the greatest flexibility and interesting activity are often those that are least available. Flexible new structures, workplace options, and additional resources are needed from the public, private, and non-profit sectors to stimulate the creation of new work opportunities and enterprises that will be responsive to the needs, interests, and expectations of Baby Boomers.

Table 1. Range of Productive Aging Opportunities

- Continue with existing job or begin a new job on a full-time basis
- Negotiate a phase-down in the number of working hours
- Arrange for consulting or project work
- Accept a telecommuting job
- Create arts, literature, or science intellectual property for future compensation
- Take a part-time position or seasonal work
- Take a compensated volunteer position
- Volunteer with an organization
- Become a caregiver
- Start a non-profit organization
- Create a new business
- Retrain for a new career, trade, or occupation

Understandably, most of the attention of policy makers has been devoted to two sectors–paid work and volunteering. In 2005, Senator Herb Kohl (D-Wisconsin) proposed an "Older Worker Opportunity Act" to begin the process of exploring ways government can be more supportive and less structured regarding work and volunteering opportunities for older Americans. Kohl states:

> A one-size-fits-all retirement will no longer match the very different plans that seniors and baby boomers have for their later years. Rethinking retirement is also vital to our nation's economic future. By 2030, businesses could face a labor shortage of 35 million workers, and the projected slowdown in labor force growth could translate into lower economic growth and living standards (Senate Bill 1826, 2005).

Members of Congress and constituent organizations have been vocal about the need to plan and respond to the inevitable demographic shifts facing the nation. However, despite the prevalence and urgency of the issue, too little innovation or policy response has occurred. In a series of studies conducted by the Urban Institute, Zedlewski and Butrica estimate that there is currently a large population of able older adults who are not working or volunteering–the estimated number of individuals exceeds 10 million people and, as we look to the future, this number will continuously grow larger (Zedlewski and Butrica, 2007). The cost for this lost human productivity not only affects the nation, but it may not be what older people seek for themselves.

And for most, including older individuals, it is hard to make new connections, to find new jobs, or to create new opportunities. For some, work in late life needs to be more than a way to pass time or earn income; it needs to have meaning and purpose, and not all jobs or volunteer roles provide such opportunities. Carstensen (1992) has pointed out that many older people pass up opportunities to be engaged in productive activity. With full recognition of their phase in life, many older people become highly selective with what they will become involved, choosing those activities that will make best use of their time and talents. Some activities that require new associations may require more energy and investment than the older individual is willing to give at this time of life. It has also been noted that many of the tasks volunteers are asked to do in non-profit organizations are the same as those offered to previous generations of volunteers and may not provide the challenge expected by a new cohort of potential volunteers. And so we have a call for more meaningful work opportunities in volunteering and civic engagement, and modest change to accommodate these needs and interests.

What is Missing?

There are certainly examples of ways in which companies have attracted or retained older workers. Each year AARP provides awards to the 50 best companies for older workers, and yet the fundamental paradigm of employer-employee relations remains largely unchanged. Although we acknowledge the efforts of companies to attract and retain older workers, innovative and creative approaches remain extremely limited. Programs in Japan such as the Silver Human Resource Centers (SHRC), on the other hand, have provided a fresh and novel approach to the role of government and the private sector in fostering new industries and roles for its senior citizens (Bass, 1994). Other creative approaches to work—be it paid-volunteering, service-learning, social entrepreneurship, or volunteering designed and matched to the talents and capabilities of older people—remain to be created in the United States.

The SHRC, initially a 1974 experiment in Edogawa Ward in Tokyo as a model for part-time contracted work, has now expanded to nearly 1000 centers nationwide. The SHRC is a community-based, non-profit corporation that provides contracted services from a labor pool of older people, something of a cross between a senior center, a jobs bank, and a sheltered workshop. The infrastructure and facility resemble that of a private company, complete with uniforms, equipment, and a fleet of vehicles. The SHRC, originally named Corporation for the Aged, was an idea shaped by Professor Kazuo Okochi, former president of Tokyo University. He describes the SHRC as the following:

> The aim of the Corporation of the Aged is not offering jobs to older people based on employment relations between employers and employees. It aims to promote voluntary work activities of older people for their own mutual assistance and cooperation in a local community. It is a movement of older people about 60 years or more looking for positive ikigai (a sense of fulfillment in life)

through work activities based on their life-long experience, skills, and wisdom in a local community (Okochi, 1989, pp. 9-10).

Members of the SHRC seek contracts with private or public organizations for services. Work done by older people is paid on a part-time hourly basis. Contracted tasks by SHRC workers might include technical jobs involving translation, tutoring, and proofreading; semi-skilled jobs such as gardening, or simple carpentry; clerical jobs; caretaking of facilities such as parks, museums, and parking locations; canvassing jobs; light manual jobs; home help and caregiving; and a variety of other work. One SHRC had jobs for members to serve as older actors for the movie industry. Funding for the SHRC facility, equipment, and infrastructure comes from national and local funds. Wages paid to the SHRC workers are derived from the contracts negotiated for services. The model has become very successful throughout the nation.

Key to the success of the SHRC are both its innovative approach that draws upon government and private sector support for start-up and its involvement of older people in its leadership, management, and operations. Older people run the SHRC for older people. It is a source of pride and provides services that are needed in the community. Older people affiliated with the SHRC have a sense of purpose and meaning in what they do and also receive some modest compensation for their work. While not formal employees, the SHRC members are also not strictly volunteers.

Older people in America are also seeking meaning in their work just like the Japanese. While no longer needing a substantial salary in many cases, there are older people who would like to have some income to offset the costs incurred for their volunteer work such as transportation and meals. Hence the notion of paid-volunteerism, which is when the individual is provided a stipend for the services rendered. This provides some recognition for the value added and reduces the out-of-pocket cost needed to provide service. This concept needs further development and expansion as a promising way to engage the larger number of Baby Boomers who will be retiring.

Most important to the success of innovations in work and volunteering is the engagement of older people themselves. These people are able to innovate, create new kinds of organizations, and foster new models of paid and partially-paid work. The success of the

SHRC is predicated on the involvement of and ownership by older people.

Missing from much of the talk is the full engagement of older people themselves in creating new approaches. Marc Freedman, founder of Civic Ventures, is one individual with an organization that is on the right course. Civic Ventures has been speaking to issues of elder empowerment and the talent that resides in the community itself. No better example exists than the Purpose Prize, for which Americans over age 60 are nominated to receive awards of $100,000 for identifying new ways to solve social problems. A total of five awards of $100,000 each are available in 2008, and another ten awards of $10,000 are also offered. Fully cognizant of the talent available, Civic Ventures has provided incentives for older people to come forward with original ideas to respond to vexing social issues.

A Call for Resources to Prime the Pump and Stimulate a New Vision for an Aging Society

For the first time, in 2008, Baby Boomers born in 1946 will be eligible for Social Security, and many more will follow in the succeeding 17 years. We are at the cusp of an age revolution, with the creative youth of the 1970s just beginning to enter their 50s and early 60s. While they are growing older, their capacity and willingness to create new institutions and foster new ideas has not abated. The 2020 equivalent of *What Color is Your Parachute?* has not been written–but it will be. The climate is right for change, the markers have been placed, the antecedents are there, and the expectations have been set.

While some Baby Boomers will continue to work in traditional organizations, many others will seek to find meaningful and perhaps novel engagement in later life. One could imagine new kinds of organizations being started and growing quickly. Just as Elderhostel has become so successful, other kinds of elder-based organizations could become commonplace. These elder-based organizations could foster opportunities for work, volunteering, service-learning, or developing communities of interest for similarly interested people. These new institutions will evolve, and many will have a founder who is "one of them."

There will be opportunities for new kinds of products and services to be created. Look how quickly the Apple i-Pod has integrated itself into modern society. Apple founder Steve Jobs was born in 1955 and is part of the Baby Boom generation. He and others like him will not stop innovating and engaging in entrepreneurial activities–they will simply grow older and benefit from their accumulated wisdom and experience. Baby Boomers will not suddenly change their persona when they turn 62, 65, or 70. Many will seek to create new services and institutions that best serve the needs they see around them.

To further tap the talent that is already there, enabling institutions are needed to play a role. The Japanese SHRC model would not exist if it were not for the role of government, providing funds for start-up costs and basic infrastructure support. In this case, the government provided a critical enabling function. In the United States, we need to take a fresh look at government, foundations, and the private sector for ways to foster new policies, programs, and incentives that engage the potential of an aging society.

Recently in the United States, the Skoll Foundation has provided an example of the kind of enabling intervention that will be needed to take advantage of the opportunities. The Skoll Foundation has established awards for Social Entrepreneurship, established a Center dedicated to the same purpose, and launched an online community to connect social entrepreneurs with resources to help support one another and respond with social action. With the wealth created by Baby Boomers, one can imagine Baby Boom philanthropists creating new organizations designed to foster original opportunities for other older people.

At the same time that some successful Baby Boomers will devote their time and resources to social causes, others will be busy continuing in their creation of new enterprises. These can be either within larger organizations or universities (intrapraneurship) or by the creation of entirely new entities. Career counseling services must be expanded to provide guidance for later–life career opportunities. New sorts of food and restaurants will appear on the horizon, and it will not be unusual for the founder to be someone who is well beyond age 60.

As mentioned, enabling institutions are critical for the realization of the aging potential. In this case enabling institutions refers to the availability of resources designed to foster the creation of new opportunities and new entities for providing meaningful and productive engagement for those who seek such opportunities. While there is sufficient human capital for a robust and productive aging society, there are limits on financial capital and structures to support such engagement. Government plays a vital role in providing tax policy, stimulus packages, funding for innovative programs, retraining support, funding for science and technology, and small business grants and loans to move the research and development innovation engine forward. Government can prime the pump to capture the imagination and creativity of the aging population, which exist in great measure despite the popular myths and stereotypes. In particular, grant programs targeted to older economic or social entrepreneurs are needed that will foster new small businesses and innovations in larger corporations, and create new non-profits and socially motivated for-profit companies.

Funds and enabling structures are needed to help creative people in their later years establish new kinds of organizations, large and small, that are personally satisfying, socially responsible, and good for the country. These funds and creative programs can come from industry, philanthropy, or government. The United States needs to recognize the benefits and opportunities of demographic change, rather than creating problems, and to begin taking advantage of them.

Shaping Our Future

The demographics are there, not for doom and gloom, but for tremendous opportunity. A large and growing pool of human capital is ready and willing to continue adding value. In the coming years, the transition from being part of the workforce to being labeled retired or even elderly will be less visible, less categorical, and less demarcated than in the past. It is possible to foster innovation, economic growth, and social responsibility as we plan for tomorrow and beyond. We need to leave the old models of retirement and even volunteerism behind and to foster a world where older workers are utilized to a substantially greater extent.

Matilda White Riley and her colleagues (1994) had it right when they indicated that our social institutions lag behind our culture. Our institutions are invested in structures, policies, and practices of the past, which are simply unresponsive to the challenges and opportunities before us. We can reshape a modern society, and the time is now.

Productive Aging

Robert N. Butler, M.D., Ph.D.

Leading gerontologist; President and Chief Executive Officer International Longevity Center-U.S.; first Director; National Institute on Aging; and Pulitzer award-winning author.

Introduction

The world is experiencing a new kind of growth as years are added to both ends of the life course. Although the birth rate has dropped, there has been an unprecedented reduction in maternal, infant, childhood, and late life mortality rates. People are also living longer, and by 2030, twenty percent of the population will be 65 and older.

The rise in the number of older people will have lasting effects on society. The aging population is already affecting the global economy. In the same way that the 1960s had a youth market that targeted the baby boomer generation, today there is a growing mature market, called the "silver industries" in Japan, that focuses on serving the needs of the older population. The growth of the mature market has prompted an economic boom in many industries, including health care, pharmaceutical, financial services, tourism, and recreational industries.

The picture of later life itself has changed. It is no longer a portrait of passivity, senility, and sexlessness. Today, older people are active, vigorous, and intellectually robust. Studies conducted at the National Institutes of Health and at Duke University in the 1950s concluded that many of the stereotypes attributed to the aging process are actually a consequence of disease, social adversity, and even of personality. These studies opened the door to the possibility that aging itself was mutable. We began to understand the underlying mechanisms of aging itself, for example Leonard Hayflick's important finding that a cell replicates a limited number of times before dying.

Before the 21st century is over, biological and societal advancement by gene-based and regenerative medicine will further extend longevity. The demographic changes will necessitate new work patterns, including significant roles for older Americans, both in the paid and voluntary sectors. The 21st century will become the century of productive old age.

A Brief Historical Perspective

The world has experienced three waves of longevity: Fossil evidence from between two and a half million and one hundred thousand years ago suggests the size of the cranium doubled, as did the length of life as hominids evolved to homo sapiens.

Twelve thousand years ago, during the Neolithic period, animal husbandry and agriculture became established and brought a greater abundance of food. Humankind no longer had to survive as hunter-gatherers. At the same time, a greater density of human settlements created closer contact with animals and insect vectors, and therefore with diseases. The average life expectancy may have been about 20 years.

Between 1900 and 2000, the average life expectancy in the industrialized world increased by nearly 30 years, and it continues to rise today. The enormity of that achievement can best be appreciated by considering that life expectancy increased by only 27 years in the 4500-year span between the Bronze Age and the year 1900.

Beginning in the 17th century, the Industrial Revolution witnessed major increases in longevity. In 1776, the average American colonist lived to 35. By 1900 the average American lived to 47. As of 2005 figures, that number has increased to nearly 78 and is still rising. There has been a 60 percent drop in deaths from cardiovascular diseases and stroke since 1950, as well as significant decreases in disability rates. Historical demographers point out that in 1830 approximately one out of three newborn infants survived to 60 years of age. Today, eight out of ten will reach 60.

In all of history, half of all human beings who have turned 65 are living today.

In the 21st century, we are likely to experience a fourth wave of longevity. Effective biomedical research and new discoveries about retarding the processes of aging will enable us to live better as well as longer. Since people are living longer, they will work longer, which will in turn prompt changes in the American workplace. Society at all levels will be challenged to develop ways to promote productive aging.

Defining Productive Aging

The term "productive aging" is the capacity of an individual or population segment to serve in the paid work force and in volunteer activities, and to maintain autonomy and independence for as long as possible. Productive aging means the valuable contributions that older people make to the family, the community, and to national life. For example, foundations estimate that billions of dollars of equivalent contributions have come from older people who do volunteer work.

The concept of productive aging was developed in 1982 at a seminar in Salzburg, Austria. Herbert Gleason, James Birren, Alvar Svanborg, Betty Friedan, and I, among others, explored the variety of ways older people can continue to contribute to society.

Why Productive Aging?

In the 1950s, the sociologist Ernest Burgess wrote that older people lived "roleless" lives. **Unfortunately, that observation still holds true.** Yet, evidence suggests a cause-and-effect relationship between health, productivity, and longevity. Studies begun in 1955 by the National Institutes of Health have demonstrated that older people who have goals and structure are more likely to live longer. Health supports productivity and productivity encourages health. Productive aging would appear to be in the best interests of both society and the individual.

In some ways, retirement has been a 20th century aberration. It was required when the majority of people labored in mines, factories, and foundries, and it continues to be humane and necessary for individuals who have reasons to stop working after a lifetime of toil. The current trend toward early retirement is partly a reflection of a rising demand for leisure as our society becomes more prosperous. It also reflects the disincentives created by private pension rules to discourage workers from remaining in the workforce after they reach 65.

Given that our life expectancy has risen substantially since the passage of Social Security in 1935, there is no logical reason why people must automatically retire at 65. When baby boomers begin to turn 65 in 2011, many will retire. Urban Institute Senior Fellow Rudolph Penner notes, "What we are about to witness, if existing patterns are maintained, is the putting to pasture of unprecedented percentages of productive adults of this nation. In relative terms, the decline in the employment rate for adults is on the order of the increase in employment that took place during the Great Depression, only this time the change is scheduled to be permanent."[1] These very experienced workers will be forced out of the workplace, some into part-time and consultant positions.[2] *It seems absurd that some 78 million people, with their education and talent, should cease contributing to society for as long as 30 years.*

How to Promote Continuing Productivity

Older workers represent a reservoir of talent and experience. How can we alter the work place and work tasks to accommodate their changing physiology in order to maximize the opportunity for continuing contributions? The upcoming generations of older persons will require innovative adjustments if they are to remain productive. These will include retraining to enable older workers to keep abreast of technological advances, and job sharing, which would allow older workers to reduce their working hours while maintaining a portion of their income. It is also likely that many older workers will want to work from home or become self-employed. Employment programs for older Americans should include computer centers to enable communities to match the skills of volunteers and paid older workers with areas of need.

Blue collar workers pose a special challenge. As they age, these workers may no longer be up to the physical rigors of their jobs. In some cases, blue collar workers who want to remain on the job may be retrained to do other jobs, or their jobs may be modified to fit their changing abilities. Experienced blue collar workers may also be used to train younger workers.

There is much to learn from the experiences of other societies. Imaginative social solutions need to be developed, like Japan's system of providing employer subsidies to retain or hire older workers. In the U.S., Medicare might become the first payer of health care costs after 55 years of age, which would lower the costs of hiring older employees. Employers must be educated in the importance of continuing worker education and periodic sabbaticals to enable the workforce to upgrade skills throughout life; Australians already go on "extended service leave" sabbaticals, and Norway is considering a program of one year off every ten years so its citizens can upgrade their skills.

Investments must be made in biomedical and behavioral research and studies that help older people to compensate for age-related disabilities. Programs of health promotion and disease prevention, combined with affordable geriatrics care, will help to keep the older workforce productive. Accommodations will have to be made to reflect the specific ergonomic requirements and changing physical capabilities of older workers.

Obviously, unless jobs exist, older Americans cannot be productively employed, and unless the Age Discrimination in Employment Act of 1967 is strictly enforced, many will not be hired. Researchers at the International Longevity Center have found that older Americans are employed in a wide variety of paid occupations, but that such opportunities are limited.

The Organisation for Economic Co-operation and Development (OECD), comprised of 30 member countries, has advocated that people remain active and work longer. It has noted that, "whereas in 1960 men lived approximately 68 years, of which 50 years were spent in paid employment, today men live to 76 with only 38 years spent in paid employment. If the trend continues, by 2020 men will spend significantly more of their lives outside the workforce than they do as paid employees."[3]

Benefits to Employers

Employers have good reason to adapt to the needs of older workers. While physical powers diminish with age and older workers may be slower at some tasks, research suggests that they are better problem solvers. They may deliberate before making decisions, but they tend to be right more often than younger employees. In some cases, workers over 65 have the best performance record of any age group. They are much less likely to suffer occupational injuries than younger workers, and are more likely to complete on-the-job training and to remain with their employer.[4] Studies by ICF Kaiser International and the AARP have shown that older workers are usually more reliable than younger employees and miss work less often. Older workers are also more experienced and demonstrate maturity and good judgment.

Intergenerational Conflict or Collaboration?

The longevity revolution has completely transformed the relationship between generations. Some pundits believe that this sets up a battle between the generations, but Harris Polls completed in 1998 and 2000 contradict this view.[5] Humphrey Taylor, Chairman of the Harris Poll, reported that: "The picture which emerges from these data...is one of remarkable harmony and agreement between different generations, and a marked lack of intergenerational conflict."[6]

Nick Vanston noted that if older workers do not continue to contribute to society, sometime after 2010 there is likely to be a reduced growth in material standards of living, with fewer workers to support more retirees. This in turn will raise fiscal and intergenerational fairness issues.

The Future of Productive Aging

What is the year 3000 going to bring? With the decrease in the birth rate, older workers will be needed to do the work of society. Undoubtedly, it will prompt changes in the American workplace. In the future, some people are likely to want to continue to work because of financial need, while others will do so because they enjoy working.

Retirement may change, with increased emphasis on phased retirement, which would allow workers to gradually cut down their working hours as they get older, and of trial retirements, which would allow workers to return to their job if they change their mind and decide not to retire after all. Sweden has already experimented with both phased and trial retirements.

Perhaps people will work a 30-hour work week until they are 90, with many choosing to work at home. A National Youth Community Service would delay entry into the workforce. Everyone would take a sabbatical and multiple careers and extended work lives would become customary.

Conclusion

In 1900, Americans could realistically expect to live to about age 47. Their normal workweek was 60 hours, and their economic safety net virtually nonexistent. In 2005 the average life expectancy was nearly 78 years. Americans today have a 40-hour workweek, with a minimum wage, Medicare, and Social Security—to say nothing of computers, automobiles, air conditioners, air travel, and much more.

The times have changed, and it is time to begin viewing older people, individually and collectively, as a valuable resource to meet their own and society's needs. People over 65 are responsible for developing their productive potential to the fullest extent possible: to work for pay, to serve family and community, to share artistic and avocational abilities, and to maintain themselves independently for as long as is feasible. Older people can remain productive by understanding health promotion, disease prevention, and methods of compensating for disability.

Society should be responsible for providing a fair share of the educational, environmental, health care, and other resources that enable individuals to age productively. Older people must be encouraged to continue to utilize a lifetime of thinking and experience, with opportunities for mentoring, modeling, and teaching.

Older people can put the experiences of a lifetime at the disposal of our society in a variety of ways. We cannot afford to waste their valuable talents and capabilities.

Converging Forces Require Action

William K. Zinke

President of Human Resource Services, Inc., a consulting firm he organized in 1969 to focus on human resources management, which has created and funded the Center for Productive Longevity

We have mentioned the convergence of forces elsewhere in the book, and it may be helpful to state them as a predicate for discussing the required action.

Projected Talent Shortages

We read about labor shortages, but the real shortages relate to talent (i.e., the knowledge, skills and ability to satisfy job requirements). This talent shortage has been projected at four-ten million by 2010, and more thereafter as Baby Boomers reach retirement age. Whatever the actual numbers, the reality is that the U.S. is facing an aging and shrinking workforce: shrinking because of lower birth rates and aging because we have 78 million Baby Boomers, the oldest of whom reach early retirement age of 62 in 2008 and each year thereafter through 2025 at 4.28 million per year).

The projected talent shortages can result in diminished productivity gains, economic growth, and the ability of American companies to compete in global markets.

A Large and Growing Talent Pool

Nobody has developed a better word for retirement, despite many attempts including rewirement and rehirement. However, the Rs apply because, with 30 years added to longevity during the 20th Century, many workers 55+ who have terminated regular career jobs want to continue working as a way of renewal, regeneration and revitalization. Graduating students receive a commencement address; many older workers see this as a time of re-commencement.

In recent surveys, 80 percent of the Baby Boomers indicate that they intend to continue working after terminating their regular career jobs, a majority in part-time versus full-time positions. The reasons range from needing or wanting the additional income to a variety of factors that relate to satisfaction with life (see Appendix 4).

At a time when the U.S. is facing a second energy crisis–the lack of human energy required to maintain our productivity gains and economic growth–employers have the benefit of a large and growing talent pool of workers 55+ with experience, expertise, seasoned judgment and proven performance who are ready and qualified to continue in productive activities.

Restated, what we have in America is a true convergence of forces: increasing talent shortages and a growing talent pool of workers 55+ who are ready and qualified to continue adding value. The cover of this book symbolizes these two forces and the need to build bridges that will facilitate their convergence.

Required Action

The Need for Flexible Workplace Options

In the paid-employment area, which relates to the private, public, and non-profit sectors, there is increasing recognition of the need to develop flexible workplace policies/practices and compensation packages that will retain and attract workers 55+ who can continue to add value. These options range from phased retirement to various forms of part-time work to work on a project basis (see Appendix 5). Compensation packages may need to be individually tailored, with a salary that may be the same or less than the worker's previous pay and benefits that include some form of healthcare coverage because it is frequently desired. According to the BLS, the work participation rate of people 55 to 64 is 63.4 percent for 2007 and projected at 67.0 percent in 2020. Providing flexible workplace options can increase participation rates and therefore reduce talent shortages.

Employers should also increase their training programs for workers 55+, more carefully monitor practices that result in age discrimination, and improve their training programs for managers and supervisors on managing a multi-generational workforce that will include a larger number of workers 55+.

Changes in Laws, Regulations and Public Policy

At the federal level, the U.S. Department of Labor (DoL) and other agencies have failed to take necessary action. The DoL has been urged by the U.S. Government Accountability Office (GAO) since 2000 to organize an interagency task force to consider what changes are required to eliminate the impediments that discourage employers from retaining or recruiting older workers and that also discourage older workers from continuing in employment. Finally, such a task force was launched in May 2006 with senior representatives from nine federal agencies: the Departments of Commerce, Education, Health and Human Services, Labor, Transportation, and Treasury plus the Equal Employment Opportunity Commission, Small Business Administration, and Social Security Administration.

Its report, issued in February 2008, had some useful information but contained this statement on required legal and regulatory changes: "Strategies include further policy exploration of legal and regulatory issues by an interagency group, and research on specific issues to determine whether changes are needed to current laws and regulations." Rather than "further policy exploration", since the legal and regulatory issues are well known and have been stated frequently, the time has come for action rather than further exploration. Impetus from Congress, the private and non-profit sectors would be helpful in this regard.

Financially Unsustainable Social Programs

There is growing awareness and genuine concern about the financial unsustainability of our social programs, particularly Social Security and Medicare. With the advent of prescription drug coverage, Medicare accounted for 8.4 percent of GDP in 2007 and is projected at 14.5 percent in 2030.[1]

With the retirement age of Social Security increasing at a glacially slow rate to 67 by 2022 and healthcare costs escalating, the question is how long our social programs can continue without major changes.

One obvious change is to increase the retirement age to 70 from 65, which was the age established by the Social Security Act in 1935, on a more rapid but equitable basis and then index it to further longevity gains that are bound to occur. Other tenable proposals include a "means test" for Social Security benefits, require workers to save for their retirement, and increase the base on which taxes are paid. The time has come to confront the challenge of changing our social programs before we are required to deal with the problems and potential crises.

Unprecedented Talent Shortages in the Public Sector

At the federal level, where the average workforce age is more than seven years higher than the private sector, there is increasing recognition of looming talent shortages but limited action to deal with the problem. The civil service has far more employees over age 45 than the private sector (58% vs. 41%).

The impact on government effectiveness is increased by the concentration of tenure in senior management and supervisory roles. By 2012, 36 percent of the Senior Executive Service Corps will retire, and eligibility for retirement may be as high as 76 percent. At the supervisory level, projected retirement by 2012 is 27 percent.[2]

These challenges can be alleviated by private, public and non-profit collaboration that is already developing. The non-profit Partnership for Public Service has developed a collaborative project with the U.S. Office of Personnel Management and IBM to train employees approaching retirement for positions with the U.S. Treasury Department. This is a pilot project that can lead to staffing other federal agencies and could serve as an excellent stimulus for meeting the emergent talent needs in the public sector.

National Campaign to Change the Mindset About Aging and Retirement

The country needs a national campaign to change the mindset about aging and retirement because there is an entrenched belief that when you reach a certain age (perhaps 55 and certainly 60), you are "over the hill", "on the shelf", and "out of the game". Despite the reality that age is no longer a determinant of ability to add value, ageism (loosely defined as negative thinking about older people) continues to have a pervasive impact. It is past time that we respected and appreciated the experience, expertise and "business intelligence" of older workers. A quotable saying is that: "Good judgment comes from experience, and experience comes from bad judgment".

Surveys document that workers 55+ are more reliable and dependable, are more committed and dedicated to their work, have much lower absenteeism and turnover, and have better overall skills and abilities than younger workers. The average job tenure in 2006 for workers 18 to 35 in service companies was 2.9 years compared with 9.3 years for workers 55+. With growing talent shortages, there will be more competition for younger workers and shorter job tenures, which should stimulate companies to invest substantially more in the training and development of older workers.

Change in the Attitudes and Expectations of Older Workers

Older workers have become acculturated to believe in the traditional meaning of retirement with reliance on a pension, Social Security and other entitlement programs, and their savings to support their post-retirement years. Many do not fully realize that they may be living 20 to 30 years longer than they expected and that they will be more responsible for rising healthcare costs including long-term care. In the current economic downturn, they have been confronted with reduced value of their homes, in most cases their principal asset, and higher costs for basic items like gasoline and food.

It is important for this population segment to develop life management plans to accommodate these changes. This may entail development of a plan of action either to remain in the workforce or to seek employment; an alternative would be to create their own business or to become independent contractors.

A life management plan would extend beyond finances to setting goals and objectives for how to enjoy their expanded longevity. The three essential elements for successful aging are productive engagement, social connection and physical fitness.[3] A commitment to these three factors can contribute to an enhanced quality of life.

Conclusion

The following BLS chart dramatically demonstrates the need for change. It shows that the projected labor force increase for workers 65 and over is 84 percent from 2006 to 2016 and 37 percent for workers 55 to 64. It also projects limited growth of only 15 percent over that ten-year period for workers 25 to 34.

Labor force change by age group

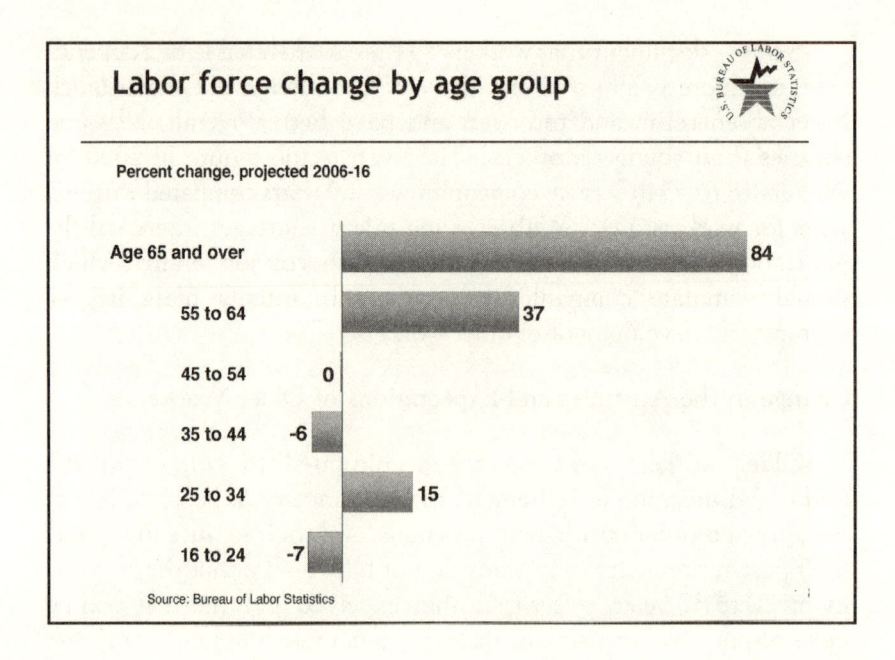

Percent change, projected 2006-16

Age group	% change
Age 65 and over	84
55 to 64	37
45 to 54	0
35 to 44	-6
25 to 34	15
16 to 24	-7

Source: Bureau of Labor Statistics

It is clear that employers need to place more emphasis on strategic workforce planning and to ensure its integration with strategic business planning. An important component is to ascertain the number of people in senior management roles and mission-critical positions who are five-ten years from retirement and what are their retirement plans. Another important component is to develop systems for transferring or capturing the "business intelligence" of key people before they retire.

This planning should cover the entire workforce and attracting/retaining the talent needed to support the company's four Ps: people, productivity, performance and profitability. This will entail retaining older workers for longer periods of time where they are ready and qualified to continue adding value; tapping this large and growing talent pool of workers 55+ to a substantially greater degree; and developing a range of flexible workplace options to retain and attract older workers.

Gary Becker, a Professor at the University of Chicago and a Nobel Laureate, wrote a column for Business Week in a January 2000 issue, titled "Longer Life Was the Century's Greatest Gift". A gift is something to be used and appreciated. It is time that employers substantially increase their utilization of workers 55+ and recognize their ability to contribute to our economic and social well-being.

Winston Churchill once said: "A pessimist sees the difficulty in every opportunity; an optimist sees the opportunity in every difficulty". There are many difficulties in confronting the economic and social impact of demographic change, both in the U.S. and in other industrialized countries around the world. But if we seize the benefits and opportunities detailed in Appendix 2, there is no question that we can maintain a strong, vibrant economy and society. The converging forces will be an essential element in achieving this result.

Notes and References

Preface: A Personal Journey
William K. Zinke

1. Financial Times, May 30, 2007

The Challenges and Opportunities of Demographic Change
The Honorable David M. Walker

1. Without any changes, this will fall to 70 cents of every dollar of promised benefits in 2081.
2. GAO-08-8, Nov. 29, 2007
3. GAO-06-80, Dec. 5, 2005
4. GAO-05-325SP, Feb. 1, 2005

Live Longer, Work Longer: An OECD Perspective on Ageing and Employment Policies in the United States
John P. Martin

1. For details, see OECD (2007), Part II
2. In this paper, older workers are defined as all workers aged 50 and over. The age of 50 is not meant to be a watershed in and of itself in terms of defining who is old and who is not, but it does correspond to the age after which labour force participation rates begin to decline in most OECD countries.
3. Further details on the other recommendations can be found in OECD (2005)
   OECD (2005), Ageing and Employment Policies: United States, Paris
   OECD (2006), Live longer, Work longer, Paris
   OECD (2006 b), Sickness, Disability and Work: Breaking the Barriers–Norway, Poland and Switzerland, Paris
   OECD (2007), Pensions at a Glance: Public Policies across OECD countries, Paris

The New Retirement: Myths and Models
Helen Dennis, M.A.

1. Bennis, W. (October 1995). Reflections on retirement. *Vital Speeches* Vol. LXI, No.24
2. Pollan, S.M. & Levine, M. (1995). The rise and fall of retirement. *Worth.* 65-74
3. National Endowment for Financial Education (1999). Retirement

planning for the 21st century. CO: National Endowment for Financial Education. p. 21-22
4. Bronte, L. (1993). *The Longevity Factor*. NY: HarperCollins
5. Butler, R.N. & Gleason, H.P. (1985). Opportunities: A dialogue between Betty Friedan and Maurice Lazarus. *Productive Aging*. p. 77-85
6. Dychtwald, K. & Flower, J. (1989). *Age Wave*. CA: Jeremy P. Tarcher
7. Goldberg, B. (2000). *Age Works*. NY: The Free Press. p. 39
8. Bratter, B. & Dennis, H. (2008). *Project Renewment: The First Retirement Model for Career Women*. New York: Scribner
9. Sedlar, J. & Miners, R. (2003). *Don't Retire, Rewire!* Indianapolis, IN: Alpha
10. Dychtwald, K., Erickson, T., Morison, B. (2004). "It's Time to Retire Retirement." *Harvard Business Review*
11. Greenwald, M. & Associates. (1997). *Longevity and Retirement Study*. Washington, DC: Greenwald & Associates
12. Ibid. 31
13. Based on the author's experience with over 10,000 mid-life employees
14. Atchley, R., *The Sociology of Retirement*. Cambridge: Schenkman Publishing, 1976
15. AARP-Roper Starch Worldwide. (1999). *Baby Boomers Envision Their Retirement: An AARP Segmentation Analysis. Executive Summary*. Washington, D.C.: AARP
16. Reingold, J. & Brady, D. (September 20, 1999). Brain Drain, *Business Week*. p. 113-128
17. Ibid. 113
18. Internet job opportunities for older workers–*U.S. News and World Report*. May 15, 2008
    DinosaurExchange.com: Lists short- and long-term job opportunities for what it terms "dinosaurs" (retirees with experience), including consultant and management positions all over the world, some in developing countries
    Enrge.us: The Employment Network for Retirement Government Experts assists retired federal, state, and local government employees with continued employment
    ExecSearches.com: Connects experienced nonprofit, government, education, and health workers with executive, mid-level, and fundraising positions
    Execunet.com: Executives who make over $100,000 annually can network with like-minded professionals and talk to recruiters
    Jobs4Point0.com: Focuses on job seekers ages 40 and over
    RetiredBrains.com: Offers nationwide job listings searchable by industry or state

RetireeWorkForce.com: Hosts virtual job fairs as well as job postings and résumé services
RetirementJobs.com: Certifies employers as offering a friendly work environment for older workers
Seniors4Hire.org: Seniors can apply for jobs, submit résumés, or post a description of their ideal job
ThePhoenixLink.com: This nonprofit group connects experienced executives and technologists with short- and long-term management positions
WorkForce50.com: Lists jobs exclusively from employers who are enthusiastic about hiring workers over age 50
YourEncore.com: Connects retired scientists, engineers, and others

19. M. Bendick, L.E. Brown, and K.Wall. "No Foot in the Door: an Experimental Study of Employment Discrimination Against Older Workers," Journal of Aging and Social Policy, 12.4 (1999): p. 5-23
20. http://www.lifeplanningnetwork.org
21. http://www.womansage.org
22. http://www.thetransitionnetwork.org/AboutUs.aspx
23. www.ProjectRenewment.com
24. Dennis, H. (Spring 1994). The Changing Work Environment: Messages for the Mature. *Career Planning and Adult Development Journal*
25. Dennis, H. & Axel, H. (1991). *Encouraging Employee Self-Management in Financial and Career Planning*. NY: The Conference Board, Report # 976
26. Dennis, H. (1993). The Increasing Need for Self-Management. In *Working with Older Workers*. (Editors: R. Schwartz & B. Ryan)
27. Dennis, H. (Spring 1994). The Changing Work Environment: Messages for the Mature. *Career Planning and Adult Development Journal*
28. Greenwald, M. & Associates, Employee Benefit Research Institute & American Savings Education Council. (1999). *1999 Women's Retirement Confidence Survey*. Washington, DC
29. Ibid
30. E-Learning Strategies for Executive Education. (May 15, 2000). *Fortune Magazine*. S10
31. Personal conversations with corporate decision makers
32. http://www.lifeplanningnetwork.org/find-consultant.htm
33. Handy, C. (1990). *Age of Unreason*. Boston, MA: Harvard Business School Press

The Role of Enabling Institutions in Tapping the Potential of an Aging America
Scott A. Bass, Ph.D.

AARP (2003). *Staying ahead of the curve: The AARP work and career study.* Washington, DC: AARP

AARP (2005). *Reimagining America, AARP's blueprint for the future.* Washington, DC: AARP

Bass, S.A. (1994). *Productive aging and the role of older people in Japan: New approaches for the United States.* New York: Japan Society, Inc. & International Leadership Center on Longevity and Society

Bass, S.A. (1995). *Older and active: How Americans over 55 are contributing to society.* New Haven: Yale University Press

Barth, M.C., McNaught, W., and Rizzi, P. (1995). Older Americans as workers. In S.A. Bass (Ed.). *Older and active: How Americans over 55 are contributing to society* (pp. 35-70). New Haven: Yale University Press

Campbell, J.C. (1992). *How policies change.* Princeton University Press

Carstensen, L.L. (1992). Social and emotional patterns in adulthood: Support for socioemotional selectivity theory. *Psychology and Aging, 7,* p. 331-338

Congressional Budget Office (2004). *Disability and retirement: The early exit of baby boomers from the labor force.* Washington, DC: U.S. Government Printing Office

D'Amico, C. and Judy, R.W. (1997). *Workforce 2020: Work and Workers in the 21st Century.* Indianapolis: Hudson Institute

Dannefer, D. (2003). Cumulative advantage/disadvantage and the life course: Cross-fertilizing age and social science theory. *Journal of Gerontology,* 58B, S327-S337

Freedman, M. (2007). *Encore: Finding work that matters in the second half of life.* New York: Public Affairs

GovTrack.us. S. 1826–109th Congress (2005). *Older Worker Opportunity Act.* GovTrack.us (database of federal legislation) Retrieved Feb 8, 2008 from http://www.govtrack.us/congress/bill.xpd?bill=s109-1826

Moody, H.R. (1988). *Abundance of life: Human development policies for an aging society.* New York: Columbia University Press

Morrow-Howell, N., Hinterlong, J., and Sherraden, M. (2001). *Productive aging: Concepts and challenges.* Baltimore: Johns Hopkins University Press

Okochi, K. (1989, March). "A Memorandum on the Ground Plan (May 1982) of the Tokyo Municipal Foundation for the Promotion of Undertakings for the Aged." In National Silver Human Resources Association (Ed.), *Living in an Aging Society,* a Digest of Speeches by Kazuo Okochi (pp.9-10). Tokyo: National Silver Human Resources Association

Riley, M.W., Kahn, R.L., and Foner, A. (Eds.) (1994). *Age and Structural Lag: Society's Failure to Provide Meaningful Opportunities in Work, Family and Leisure*. New York: John H. Wiley & Sons

Rowe, J.W. and Kahn, R.L. (1998). *Successful Aging*. New York: Pantheon Books

U.S. Bureau of Labor Statistics (2004). *Employment and earnings, January 1986 to January 2004* Washington, DC: U.S. Department of Labor, Bureau of Labor Statistics

U.S. Bureau of Labor Statistics (2007). Employment status of the civilian noninstitutional population by age, sex, race. Washington, DC: U.S. Department of Labor, Bureau of Labor Statistics Retrieved February 13, 2008, from http://www.bls.gov/cps/cpsaat3.pdf

Zedlewski, S.R. and Butrica, B.A. (2007, December). *Are we taking full advantage of older adults' potential?* (Urban Institute, Report Number 9). Abstract retrieved Feb 8, 2008, from http://www.urban.org/UploadedPDF/411581_adult_potential.pdf

Zinke, W.K. and Tattershall, S. (2000). *Working through Demographic Change: How Older Americans Can Sustain the Nation's Prosperity*. Boulder, Colorado: Human Resource Services, Inc.

Productive Aging
Robert N. Butler, M.D., Ph.D.

1. http://www.urban.org/news/tuesdays/12-98/penner.html
2. http://www.harrisinteractive.com/harris_poll/index.asp?PID=19
3. Vanston, N. *Longevity and Quality of Life: Opportunities and Challenges*. Ed. R.N. Butler and C. Jasmin. New York: Kluwer Academic/Plenum Publishers, 2000. p. 258
4. Lazarus M and Lauer H. *Productive Aging: Enhancing Vitality in Later Life*. Ed. R.N. Butler and H. Gleason. New York: Springer Publishing, 1985, p. 47-75
5. http://www.ilcusa.org
6. Taylor, H. *Longevity and Quality of Life: Opportunities and Challenges*. Ed. R. N. Butler and C. Jasmin. New York: Kluwer Academic/Plenum Publishers, 2000. p. 209
7. Vanston, N. *Longevity and Quality of Life: Opportunities and Challenges*. Ed. R.N.Butler and C. Jasmin. New York: Kluwer Academic/Plenum Publishers, 2000. p. 257

Converging Forces Require Action
William K. Zinke

1. The Heritage Foundation, Backgrounder, March 12, 2008
2. Partnership for Public Service, Issue Brief, May 6, 2008
3. Rowe, J.W. & Kahn, R.L. (1999), *Successful Aging*: Dell Publishing

About the Authors

Scott A. Bass, Ph.D.

Scott Bass became the Provost and Chief Academic Officer of American University in Washington, DC effective July 1, 2008. He provides leadership for AU's six schools and colleges and for the University Library, the Washington Semester Program, AU Abroad, the Center for Teaching Excellence, the Office of Enrollment, the Office of Institutional Research and Assessment, Sponsored Programs, the Office of the Registrar, and the Career Center.

Dr. Bass was previously associated with the University of Maryland, Baltimore County (UMBC) since 1996, successively serving as Dean of the Graduate School and Vice President for Research (1996-2002), Dean of the Graduate School and Vice Provost for Research and Planning (2002-2006), and Vice President for Research and Dean of the Graduate School (2005-present). His position entailed overall responsibility for setting the vision and direction for graduate education and research. He has also served as Distinguished Professor, Sociology and Public Policy (1996-present), responsible for instruction about issues in aging and social policy to graduate and undergraduate students.

Previously, Dr. Bass was associated with the University of Massachusetts Boston (UMB) from 1979-1996 as Professor, College of Public and Community Service (1990-1996), Founding Director, Gerontology Institute (1984-1996), and Graduate Director of the Ph.D. Program in Gerontology (1989-1995).

Dr. Bass has been a Visiting Professor at the School of Medicine, Stanford University and at other graduate institutions. He has also written numerous book chapters and articles on aging, retirement, productive aging, and social policy, and is the author or co-author of eight books including *Challenges of the Third Age: Meaning and Purpose in Later Life* (Oxford University Press, 2002) and *Older and Active: How Americans Over 55 are Contributing to Society*. (Yale University Press, 1995).

Robert N. Butler, M.D., Ph.D.

Robert Butler is the President and Chief Executive Officer of the International Longevity Center–U.S. (1997-present), and Professor of

Geriatrics, Henry L. Schwartz Department of Geriatrics and Adult Development, Mount Sinai School of Medicine (1995-present). In 1982, he founded the nation's first department of geriatrics at the Mount Sinai School of Medicine, where he served as Chairman and Brooksdale Professor of Geriatrics until 1995; and he served as the first Director, National Institute on Aging, National Institutes of Health (1970-1982).

Dr. Butler has had a long and distinguished career in the fields of geriatrics and gerontology, during which he has received many honors and awards. He is the author or co-author of numerous articles, book chapters, and books. In 1976 he won the Pulitzer Prize for his book *Why Survive? Being Old in America*.

Dr. Butler's Board memberships include: Kronos Longevity Research Center, Progena Research Foundation, Institute for the Study of Aging (Lauder Foundation), Americans for Healthy Aging, and American Association for International Aging. He has lectured widely around the world on issues relating to aging and productive living.

Helen Dennis, M.A.

Helen Dennis is a nationally recognized leader on issues of aging, employment, and retirement. She has conducted research on these issues for organizations such as The Conference Board, AARP, UC Berkeley, and the U.S. Administration on Aging. Nationally, she has lectured extensively to the business community, professional groups, non-profit organizations, and government agencies.

In her consulting practice, she has worked with over 10,000 employees planning for the "non-financial" aspects of their retirement including men and women who are senior executives, managers, factory workers, and university faculty and staff. As an author, she is the editor of two books, *Retirement Preparation*, and *Fourteen Steps in Managing an Aging Work Force*, and is a weekly columnist writing on successful aging for The Daily Breeze, a Media News/Hearst newspaper. Her most recent book, with co-author Bernice Bratter, is *Project Renewment: The First Retirement Model for Career Women*.

Helen Dennis has served as president of three non-profit organizations; she serves as chairperson for the American Society on Aging's Business Forum on Aging and the Healthcare and Elder Law Programs in Southern California. She was appointed as a delegate to the 2005

White House Conference on Aging and serves on the national board of the American Society on Aging.

A lecturer for more than 20 years at the University of Southern California's Andrus Gerontology Center, she has been the recipient of numerous awards for her teaching effectiveness and contributions to the field of aging.

Juhani Ilmarinen, Ph.D.

Dr. Ilmarinen has been a Professor and Director of the Theme, "Life Course and Work" at the Department of Physiology, Finnish Institute of Occupational Health (FIOH), Helsinki, Finland, since 2006. Prior to that, he was the Director from 1992 to 2005. In 1990, he served as Research Professor in the Respect for the Ageing Programme at the FIOH. Dr. Ilmarinen earned his Ph.D. in Sport Sciences (Work Physiology) at the University of Cologne, Germany.

Dr. Ilmarinen's recent work includes serving as Secretary, Scientific Committee on Ageing and Work, International Commission on Occupational Health (ICOH), 1989-2006. From 1997 to 2007, he was the Chairman, Technical Committee on Ageing, International Ergonomics Association (IEA). His activities include longitudinal studies on ageing and work, development and studies on Work Ability Index, promotion of work ability during ageing, age management, and age strategies in companies and on the national levels. He has served as an expert for the Finnish National Programme on Ageing Workers from 1998 to 2002 and for the Finnish EU-Presidency in 1999 and 2006.

Dr. Ilmarinen has made significant contributions to the fields of ageing and work ability, work physiology, ergonomics, and epidemiology, authoring more than 500 publications and eight books including, *Ageing Workers in the European Union* (FIOH, 1999) and *Towards a Longer Work Life: Ageing and Work Life Quality in the European Union* (Ministry of Social Affairs and Health, Finland, 2006).

John P. Martin

John Martin is the Director responsible for Employment, Labour, and Social Affairs at the Paris-based Organisation for Economic Co-operation and Development (OECD), which consists of 30 member countries. For two years, from 2000 to 2002, he was also Director responsible for Education before it was created as a separate OECD directorate.

Since joining the OECD in 1977, Mr. Martin has held several posts in his current Directorate and the Economics Department. He was the first editor of the *OECD Employment Outlook* from 1983 to 1986 and also edited the *OECD Economic Outlook* from 1992 to 1993. He was a Member of the Editorial Board of *OECD Economic Studies* from 1988 to 2000, and he is an Associate Editor of *Labour Economics*.

From 1996 to 1998, Mr. Martin was a member of the Visiting Scientific Committee of the Instituto di Studi per la Programmazione Economica (ISPE) in Rome. In 1997, he was a member of the committee of six independent economists who reviewed the research work and the forecasting and policy analysis of the CPB Netherlands Bureau for Economic Policy Analysis. He is a Member of the Council of the UK-based Institute for Employment Studies and a Policy Associate of the Centre for Research on Globalisation and Economic Policy (University of Nottingham). Mr. Martin is a part-time Professor at the Insititut d'Etudes Politiques de Paris (Sciences Po). He has published many articles in professional journals on topics in labour economics and international trade.

Susan R. Meisinger, SPHR

Susan Meisinger has served since March 2002 as President and Chief Executive Officer of the Society for Human Resource Management (SHRM), the world's largest association devoted to human resource management with more than 225,000 individual members in over 125 countries. Its mission is to serve the needs of HR professionals by providing the most current and comprehensive resources and to advance the profession by promoting HR's essential strategic role.

Ms. Meisinger previously held the position of Executive Vice President and Chief Operating Office of SHRM from 1999 to 2002. She also served as Senior Vice President from1997-1999 and as Vice President of Government and Public Affairs from 1987-1997.

Ms. Meisinger is a current board member for the World Federation of Personnel Management Association and the past Secretary General. She a member of the International Women's Forum and is a fellow of the National Academy of Human Resources.

Ms. Meisinger was one of the thirteen members appointed by the

U.S. Secretary of Labor to serve on the Committee on the Future of the Workplace under the President's Council on the 21st Century Workforce. She provides testimony and commentary to public policy makers, is a respected advocate on behalf of the HR profession, and frequently serves as an expert on workplace and business issues in the national media and leading publications. She is co-author of the book, *The Future of Human Resource Management*.

Humphrey J.F. Taylor

Humphrey Taylor is Chairman of the Harris Poll, a service of Harris Interactive, a leading survey research firm. He has had overall responsibility for more than 8,000 surveys in 80 countries for governments, corporations, and foundations.

Mr. Taylor has testified before congressional committees and subcommittees on Social Security, healthcare cost containment, Medicare, aging, and the taxation of employee benefits. He has published many articles and papers on survey research and public policy, and broadcasts frequently on radio and television. He writes a weekly column that is syndicated in over 100 newspapers and has written editorial page articles for leading newspapers. He has been a guest lecturer at Harvard (the Kennedy School and the School of Public Health), Oxford and New York Universities.

Mr. Taylor began his career in survey research and formed his own company, Opinion Research Centre, of which he was Chief Executive Officer from its inception until 1976, by which time it had become one of the leading British survey research organizations. In 1970, his firm was acquired by Louis Harris and Associates, and Mr. Taylor took the responsibility for building the Harris organization's international business; he moved to New York in 1976. He was appointed President of Harris in 1981, Chief Executive Officer in 1992, and Chairman in 1994.

The Honorable David M. Walker

As President and Chief Executive Officer of the Peter G. Peterson Foundation, Mr. Walker leads the Foundation's efforts to educate and activate Americans about several key challenges that threaten the country's future. These include America's budget, savings and balance of payments deficits; the need to reform existing entitlement programs; our overall health care system; and select education, energy, and non-proliferation issues.

Prior to joining the Peterson Foundation in March 2008, Mr. Walker served almost 10 years as Comptroller General of the United States and head of the U.S. Government Accountability Office (GAO). He was appointed by President Clinton and served as the federal government's chief auditor during both the Clinton and Bush (43) administrations. He previously served as a partner and global managing director of Arthur Andersen LLP and in various government and private-sector leadership positions, including presidential appointments during both the Reagan and Bush (41) administrations.

Mr. Walker also currently chairs the United Nations Independent Audit Advisory Committee. He serves on the boards of the Committee for a Responsible Federal Budget and the Partnership for Public Service, and is a Fellow of the National Academy of Public Administration. He has authored two books, is a regular commentator, and is the subject of the critically acclaimed documentary *I.O.U.S.A.* (2008). He holds a B.S. in accounting from Jacksonville University, a Senior Management in Government certificate in public policy from Harvard University's John F. Kennedy School of Government, and several honorary doctorate degrees.

William K. Zinke

William Zinke has been a management consultant since 1969 when he organized Human Resource Services, Inc. (HRS). His consulting activities have been concentrated on the human resources (HR) and legal fields, with a particular focus on strategic issues in such areas as HR planning, recruitment and selection systems, talent management and succession planning, and organizational development. Since 1999, HRS has had a major focus on the substantially increased utilization of workers 55 and older as an essential element in meeting workforce needs and sustaining the country's economic growth.

As part of his consulting activities, Mr. Zinke organized the Human Resources Roundtable Group in 1980; it consists of 65 HR heads in major North American, European, and Asia Pacific companies who meet twice yearly to focus on strategic issues relating to HR management. HRS has organized many studies, meetings, and conferences in the HR field; the latter includes events held in Brussels

(1970), Moscow (1986), Beijing (1987 and 2006), and Shanghai (2006).

Prior to founding HRS, Mr. Zinke served three years as Vice President-Industrial Relations, National Association of Manufacturers. Previously, he was a practicing attorney for more than ten years in New York City, including three years as an Assistant U.S. Attorney, Southern District of New York. He is a graduate of Amherst College and Columbia University Law School.

In Memory of Elliott Jaques, M.D., Ph.D.

Dr. Elliott Jaques, who died in 2003, was Visiting Research Professor in Management Science at George Washington University in Washington, DC. He had been engaged in practical field work over more than 50 years in the development and real-life testing of a comprehensive science-based system of organizational development and managerial leadership, including fundamental developments in our understanding of the meaning of work and in the evaluation and development of individuals engaged in work.

This work was carried out through projects in industry and commerce, in government, and in social, educational and health services including the Church of England and the U.S. Army. In the latter connection, Dr. Jaques was awarded the Joint Staff Certificate of Appreciation by General Colin Powell on behalf of the Joint Chiefs of Staff of the U.S. Armed Forces for "outstanding contributions in the field of military leadership theory and instruction to all of the service departments of the United States."

He is the author of more than 20 books, including *Requisite Organization* (1996), *Human Capability* (1994), with Kathryn Cason, and *Executive Leadership* (1991) with Stephen Clement.

Conference Sponsors

National Conference on the New Human Resources Frontier: Utilizing Older Workers for Competitive Advantage

- AEGON USA, Inc.
- Alcoa Foundation
- American Express Company
- American Federation for Aging Research
- Bank of America Corporation
- CIGNA Corporation
- Colgate-Palmolive Company
- CVS Corporation
- Genentech, Inc.
- The Home Depot, Inc.
- ING Americas
- Kirkpatrick & Lockhart Preston Gates Ellis LLP
- Merrill Lynch & Co., Inc.
- Retirement Research Foundation
- Alfred P. Sloan Foundation
- Society for Human Resource Management
- Southern Company
- Transamerica Retirement Management

The Evolution of Adulthood: A New Stage

By Dr. Elliott Jaques and William K. Zinke

An extraordinary change has taken place in industrialized countries during the past 50 years, the consequences of which have not yet been fully recognized. People are living longer and in better health, and the meaning of adult life itself has changed: a whole new stage of mature adulthood has come onto the scene, and old age has been pushed back by many years.

We propose that the onset of old age occurs much later in life and that a new stage of adulthood has emerged from 62 to 85 years of age. It is important that this phenomenon be recognized by society generally in terms of how we think about aging, retirement, and the continued involvement of older Americans in productive activities. It is even more important, however, that it be recognized by those who are in or approaching this new stage of adulthood, because it can change their lives to do so. Instead of considering themselves to be old and over the hill, they may realize that a whole new stage of active life is open to them, with untold opportunities for continued intellectual growth and accomplishment.

The facts are easy to state. Men and women are living an average of almost 18 years longer than they did in 1900, and in much better health. While many are retiring from regular full-time employment before reaching age 65, a large number of retired workers are ready, willing, and in all respects capable of working into their 60s, 70s, and 80s. They are not gerontological exceptions but fully competent adults who desire the opportunity to continue as productive contributors.

Demographic change has had a major impact on the entire world, and our thinking in America will have to catch up with that change. The retirement age of 65 was established by the Social Security Act of 1935, when average life expectancy was 61.7 years and relatively few made it past 65.[1] Today, there are almost 59 million Americans 55 and older, increasing to 75 million by 2010 and 95 million by 2020. There are 76 million baby boomers born between 1946 and 1964 who will start to join those ranks in 2001, and it has been reported that 74 to 80 percent of them plan to work in retirement.[2]

We not only need to rethink the meaning of aging and retirement in the 21st century, but there really is no alternative. Consider the following driving forces that will have an impact on future economic growth and our entire social structure:

- The U.S. population is aging, and the lower birth rates in recent years will result in a shrinking workforce.

- The oldest of the 76 million baby boomers will reach 55 in 2001 and the subsequent retirement of this group will substantially reduce workforce numbers thereafter.

- While Americans are living longer and in better health, they are retiring earlier. In 1965, 57 percent of the population over 55 was in the workforce; that figure is only 38 percent today, with many people retiring in their early 50s. Over 70 percent of Social Security recipients start drawing benefits before they reach 65.

- In 1950, there were 16.5 workers for each retiree. Today there are 3.3 workers for each retiree, and by 2030 that ratio will be reduced to almost two for each.

- In the tenth year of a strong economy, the unemployment rate has been hovering around 4 percent for most of 2000. Unemployment is projected to remain low for the next 30 years, and pockets of labor shortages have already begun to appear.

- Federal Reserve Chairman Alan Greenspan has been warning since May 1999 about the inflationary pressures that can result from low unemployment, labor shortages, and wage gains; this concern has been evidenced by substantial fluctuations in the stock market.

- Of the 59 million Americans 55 and older, a large number are retired workers who are interested in and qualified for continued employment. At a time when the country is beginning to face labor shortages, we have an enormous talent pool of people with experience, expertise, seasoned judgment and proven performance that can provide an extremely cost-effective way for companies to fill positions of particular need.

- Recent studies conducted among Human Resource professionals in companies of varying size throughout the U.S. indicate that older workers compare very favorably with younger ones in such important areas as dependability and reliability, motivation and commitment, absenteeism and turnover, and overall skills and abilities.

- As documented in the MacArthur Foundation Study of Aging in America,[3] continued productive involvement after retirement contributes to the health and well-being of older Americans.

- There is an increasing level of interest among older Americans to work in retirement, which will clearly be enhanced by the recent passage of legislation to eliminate the earnings test under Social Security for workers 65 through 69.

Need to Revise the Concept of Adulthood

The effective adult years have been regarded as comprising two stages: early adulthood from 18 to 40 and mature adulthood from 40 to 65, after which retirement begins and the "elderly" are relegated to enjoying "the golden years." That picture no longer portrays demographic realities because people are living substantially longer lives in better health.

We propose a concept of adulthood that falls into three stages:

1. First stage of early adulthood, from 18 to 40
2. Second-stage of mid-adulthood, from 40 to 62
3. New-stage of mature adulthood, from 62 to 85

Before describing this three-stage model, there are two significant points that must be made. The first is that productive activities (i.e. activities that add value) are just as important a factor for older people as for younger people in attaining a secure and balanced life. It should be clear that productive activities include continued employment for pay, entrepreneurial endeavors, various kinds of volunteer efforts, child care and elder care, and anything else that adds value to society.

We like the well-worn saying, "You don't stop having fun when you get older. You get older when you stop having fun." We do not believe that productive activities need occupy the full time of this new-stage adulthood because there should be a balance with continuous learning, time devoted to family and friends, travel and leisure activities, and whatever else contributes to making life meaningful and worthwhile for each person.

The second point is to relegate to the junkpile an almost universal belief that has been propounded by child psychologists for the past 100 years. This belief (based on research with children and adolescents but not with adults) is that human intelligence grows, increases and matures up to the age of around 18. Further **maturation** then ceases, they maintain, and all intellectual development thereafter takes place simply by learning and experience. This belief has the dysfunctional effect of giving support to the view that no further intellectual growth can occur after the age of 60 or 65 and, indeed, that we all go downhill from there.

Fifty years of research by one of the authors and his colleagues, carried out with adults in management-level work, have demonstrated that this belief is as sound as any other old wives' tale.[4] The precise opposite is the case. Their studies show conclusively that a person's potential capability (i.e. cognitive skills in action) continues to increase not only throughout childhood and adolescence but also throughout the whole of adult life up to and even beyond the age of 85 for people working at this level. This growth is a true maturation of innate human potential.

Moreover, this maturation process is predictable, as shown on the following chart, in the sense that individuals have been found to progress within their respective capability bands but not to cross over between bands. Thus, older adults will continue to mature within their bands even after retirement, so long as they remain engaged in an ordinary active life. In other words, this growth occurs at its own rate and cannot be speeded up by special educational or occupational opportunities, not does it need any such opportunities to advance. It requires only the on-going stimulus of the person's everyday life.

Growth of Potential Capability

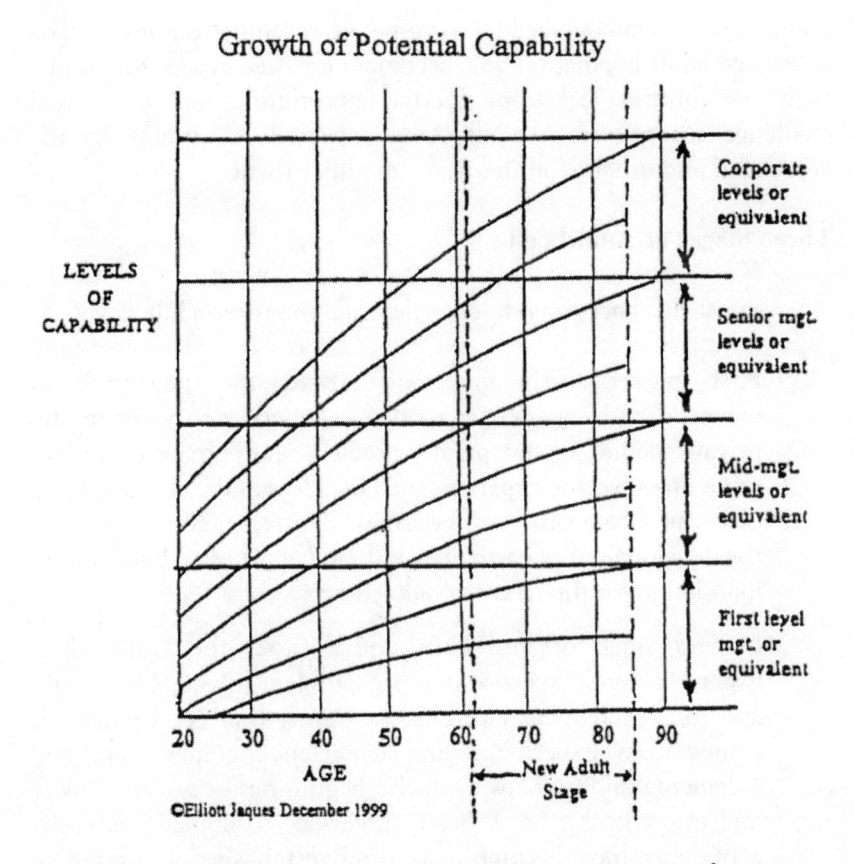

[Figure: Chart showing LEVELS OF CAPABILITY on the vertical axis against AGE (20 to 90) on the horizontal axis. Curves rise across four bands labeled (top to bottom): Corporate levels or equivalent; Senior mgt. levels or equivalent; Mid-mgt. levels or equivalent; First level mgt. or equivalent. A region from roughly age 60 to 90 is marked "New Adult Stage." ©Elliott Jaques December 1999]

These findings are of the greatest importance for a true understanding of the three stages of adulthood, particularly the new stage. The horizontal scale shows ages 20 to 90; the vertical scale shows the levels of innate potential human capability in terms of the levels of work that people will eventually be able to handle, given the necessary opportunity plus training and experience. These levels of capability are described in terms of levels of management at which a person could work if given the opportunity, or the equivalent levels for specialists and self-employed people. Individuals with the capability to work below the higher end of first-level management or its equivalent will plateau during the new stage of adulthood. A diminution of their innate ability will occur in later life only for reasons of physical deterioration.

There is thus a continuing maturational growth for many people. With the full realization of this new stage, there will be an infusion of substantial numbers of high potential capability individuals who have previously been encouraged to retire before reaching that level. The new-stage adult population will become a great economic and social asset. By contrast, lack of productive opportunities and intellectual challenge for new-stage adult Americans will contribute to the depression and other debilities that can afflict them.

Three Stages of Adulthood

Against this background, let us describe the three adult stages:

1. First stage of early adulthood (18-40)–the time to build expertise and experience; to decide whether to work in the private, public, or independent sectors and perhaps even gain some cross- sector experience; to decide whether to develop a career in a company or to become an entrepreneur; to focus on the development of particular skills and abilities; to build a solid foundation for the next two adult stages.

2. Second stage of mid-adulthood (40-62)–the time when experience and expertise produce problem-solving capabilities and sound judgment (we like the saying that good judgment comes from experience and experience comes from bad judgment) and perhaps even the beginnings of wisdom. Any mid-life crises[5] have been traversed, assurance and self-confidence have become more firmly established as a result of learning how to function more effectively, and there is continuing growth and development.

3. New-stage of mature adulthood (62-85)–the time when many individuals, although not all (e.g. people who have been engaged primarily in physical labor, who have not maintained a commitment to physical fitness, or who have debilities or disabilities), can continue to be significant contributors. They have had about 40 years to gain experience and expertise, to develop seasoned judgment and proven records of performance, to build their intellectual and social capital, and perhaps even to acquire a greater degree of wisdom. While documented research indicates that cognitive capability may have plateaued for some, the intellectual growth curve continues to move upward for people at the higher end of first-level management and above.

There is increasing evidence that many people in this new third stage, recognizing that they will be living longer and in better health, desire to remain productively engaged. One of the most important books in this field is *Successful Aging*.[6] The authors document that continuing engagement in life is an essential element in aging successfully and that most people tend to associate earning money with productive activity because compensation represents a measure of contribution. Older people who have made this transition effectively, whether their productive activity is on a paid or volunteer basis, report a greater satisfaction with life and better health. In addition, studies indicate that they live an average of four years longer than those who are not productively engaged.[7]

It is important to understand the driving forces for productive activity in this new stage of adulthood:

- The opportunity for continued intellectual stimulus and challenge

- The satisfaction and feeling of accomplishment from continuing to add value

- The desire to maintain relationships that result from working with others and the concomitant feelings of connectedness

- The ability to generate additional income either because it is necessary to maintain a standard of living or because it is desirable

- An enhanced quality of life, as well as better health and overall well being

There is nothing remarkable about delineating this new stage of adulthood. It simply confirms the demographic, economic, social and psychological realities of our changing times. People who work into their 70s, 80s, and even 90s are no longer considered to be extraordinary. What is remarkable are the embedded attitudes about aging and retirement based upon thinking that has long since become outdated and is no longer valid. We all know the stereotypical thinking:

- You can't teach an old dog new tricks.

- People who retire are over the hill and out of the game.

- Older people tend to lose their memory, and their light bulbs grow dim.
- Let's build more retirement communities so they can enjoy "the golden years."

We hear about "the aging problem," even "the aging crisis." There is so much negative thinking about getting older; bookstore shelves are stocked with titles like *Guide to Turning Back the Clock*, *Cheating Time*, and *Reversing Human Aging*. With the new realities should come an understanding and appreciation of the benefits and opportunities that result from longer life. As Nobel Prize winner Gary Becker wrote in his *Business Week* column,[8] increased longevity was the greatest accomplishment of the 20th century.

Let us think about some of the benefits and opportunities:

- We have a growing pool of almost four million Americans aged 55 and older (soon to be increased by the 76 million baby boomers) who are retired from regular full-time employment, but who are interested in and qualified for continued work at a time when we have a shrinking workforce and extremely low unemployment (perhaps we need to think about two phases: retirement and then, for the many people who want to continue working, rehirement).
- This talent pool of older workers with experience, expertise, proven performance and seasoned judgment represents a flexible and cost-effective way for companies to meet their employment needs at a time of continued low unemployment and increasing labor shortages.
- Greater utilization of new stage Americans should increase GDP, contribute to productivity gains, increase tax revenues, and help to sustain our continued economic growth and ability to compete in the global marketplace.
- Companies can maximize their return on the investment in developing the intellectual and social capital of older workers by providing them with phased retirement programs or career options that encourage those who can add value for longer periods of time to remain at work.

This last point requires further discussion. It has been suggested that retaining the talents and capabilities of older workers will impede the career growth of high-potential younger workers and may even cause intergenerational conflict. Survey research demonstrates that many older Americans want to continue to work but primarily on a part-time basis, where they can have more flexibility and less stress. Providing them with phased retirement programs and a variety of career options means that they can continue to serve as a valuable resource **without** impeding the career growth of young people.

But more needs to be said on this point. Companies make a substantial investment in developing the intellectual and social capital of their employees. By retaining their talents and capabilities for longer periods of time through special assignments or particular projects, where they can continue to add value, older workers can help companies to be more successful and to provide more jobs. Also, companies should recognize the benefits of retaining or hiring older workers where the requisite expertise is lacking within the company, particularly in these labor-short times; this would in no way impede the career growth of high-potential younger workers. Finally, retaining the services of older workers on a part-time basis can be helpful in providing training and mentoring to younger workers as they advance in their careers.

In an AARP study, the results of which were released in June 1998, 80 percent of over 2,000 baby boomers indicated that they plan to work during retirement and 17 percent of this group expect to start their own businesses.[9] We believe this trend will increase as older Americans approaching retirement understand they will be living longer and in better health, or perhaps simply because they have not saved enough to cover their retirement needs. The new businesses that are created can provide new job opportunities. It should be clear that most of the new jobs that have been created since 1982 have come from start-ups and small companies with under 20 employees (about 80 million new jobs created in such companies versus 40 million jobs lost in the downsizing of large companies).

It is past time that we redefine what we mean by aging and retirement in America. Central to this redefinition is the recognition and understanding of the new stage of adulthood. This is not a nicety–it is an absolute necessity for all Americans, including those who are moving into their new-stage years.

It is our goal to draw attention to a transformational change that is rapidly occurring throughout the world. Because of the dramatic extension of longevity, adult life in this new millennium will unfold through three stages instead of the two stages that have ended in retirement and old age. Countries around the world have received an unexpected bonus–a population segment of wise and experienced individuals ages 62 to 85 with many remaining years of vigorous and healthy life who are ready, willing, and well qualified to continue working. They will replace what has been an elderly population over 60 to 65 living out their last years in quiet retirement.

March 2000

---

[1] Datapedia of the United States (Historical Statistics of the United States from Colonial Times, 1994).

[2] *Fortune* 16 August 1999 reported the number at 74 percent, and an AARP Study entitled *Baby Boomers Look Toward Retirement* reported the number at 80 percent in June 1998.

[3] John W. Rowe and Robert L. Kahn, *Successful Aging* (1998; New York: Dell, 1999) xi-xv.

[4] Dr. Elliott Jaques and Kathryn Cason, *Human Capability* (Falls Church VA: Cason Hall & Co., 1994).

[5] Dr. Elliott Jaques, "Death and the Mid-Life Crisis," *The International Journal of Psycho-Analysis* 46.4 (1965): 502-514.

[6] op. cit.

[7] Study conducted by the Harvard School of Public Health, cited in *Denver Rocky Mountain News*, 20 August 1999.

[8] Gary S. Becker, "Longer Life Was the Century's Greatest Gift," *Business Week* 31 January 2000: 32.

[9] AARP, *Boomers Look Toward Retirement* (AARP: Washington, DC: 1998).

Benefits and Opportunities Provided by Demographic Change

- We have a growing pool of more than 10 million workers 55 and older (workers 55+) who have terminated regular career employment and are ready and qualified to continue working at a time when we have an aging, shrinking workforce with a growing war for talent.

- This pool of older workers with experience, expertise, seasoned judgment, and proven performance can be a flexible and cost-effective way for employers to meet their staffing needs at a time of growing talent shortages and a challenging business environment.

- Companies can maximize their substantial investment in the intellectual and social capital of workers 55+ by providing them with phased retirement or a variety of career options that would encourage those who can add value for longer periods of time to continue working.

- Greater utilization of workers 55+ would increase GDP, contribute to productivity gains, and help to sustain the country's economic growth and development.

- Increased employment of workers 55+ would add to tax revenues, as well as generate additional revenues for Social Security and reduce Medicare costs.

- Nationwide studies conducted among Human Resources directors document that workers 55+ compare very favorably with younger ones as to their overall skills and abilities, absenteeism and turnover, dedication and commitment to work, and reliability and dependability.

- As evidenced in The MacArthur Foundation Study of Aging in America and other research, the continued productive involvement of workers 55+ contributes to their satisfaction with life, good health, and longevity; this can have a positive effect on our entire society.

- The substantially increased utilization of workers 55+ would be specifically responsive to the needs and interests of the 78 million Baby Boomers, almost 80 percent of whom have indicated that they intend to continue working after retirement; their complete retirement would be an enormous drain on Social Security and Medicare, as well as a huge waste of human resources.

Disconnects and Dilemmas in Confronting Demographic Change

1. People are living substantially longer and in better health, but we haven't changed our thinking about aging and retirement.

2. The focus is on marketing to younger people, while older people have the money (people 55 and older own or control 70 percent of the total accumulated private wealth and account for 50 percent of total discretionary spending).

3. The views of HR executives about workers 55 and older (workers 55+) are very positive, but there is no significant emphasis on utilizing them to a substantial degree. The reality is that workers 55+ have much more to offer than younger ones in terms of experience, expertise, seasoned judgment, proven performance, and even some accumulated wisdom; research demonstrates that they also have better skills and abilities, are more reliable and dependable, and have much lower absenteeism and turnover.

4. We view people in terms of chronological age, rather than considering their overall capabilities and ability to add value.

5. Myths and stereotypes about aging are prevalent, despite a massive amount of contrary data.

6. The national focus is on removing the wrinkles and shedding the years, thus perpetuating ageism thinking and encouraging people to hide their age.

7. Companies spend much more on the training and development of younger workers than on older workers, despite the reality that investment in older people would have a better pay-off because their turnover is much lower.

8. We focus on the problems, and even crises, of an aging population without taking advantage of the benefits and opportunities.

9. The public and non-profit sectors are primarily focused on the Ds (debilities, disabilities, diseases, death) versus the Rs (renewal, revitalization, regeneration, rejuvenation), even though a greater focus on the Rs would enhance quality of life for older Americans

and lower healthcare costs (i.e., older people who remain productively engaged report greater satisfaction with life and have better health than those who don't).

10. Medicare and Social Security are financially unsustainable, and yet we only apply superficial changes.

11. Companies make a substantial investment in developing the intellectual and social capital of their employees, yet they encourage them to retire earlier or terminate them instead of obtaining a better return on that investment through providing flexible workplace options.

12. Older workers lack understanding about life management planning, but most companies don't provide counsel to employees as they approach retirement, except perhaps for financial planning.

13. Employee benefit programs, particularly defined benefit pension plans, encourage people to retire earlier, even though many would like to continue working longer.

14. Research demonstrates that millions of workers want to continue working after retirement (80% of the Baby Boomers indicate that they plan to do so), the largest percentage on a part-time basis, but most companies aren't providing phased retirement or flexible workplace options that would enable them to retain older workers who can continue adding value.

15. Laws and public policies often discourage or provide disincentives for older workers to continue in employment instead of encouraging them to do so.

16. Economic growth and our standard of living may be reduced if older Americans are not provided with opportunities to continue working (i.e., they will be drawing on savings, pension plans, and entitlement programs rather than contributing to entitlement programs, paying taxes on income, spending more money, and contributing to productivity gains and economic growth), yet there is no real recognition of the need to do so.

17. People don't start saving soon enough or in large enough amounts for their retirement needs, including long-term care, and the U.S.

continues to have an extremely low savings rate despite the fact that people are living longer.

18. More emphasis on physical fitness and regular exercise would be in the interests of older people, as well as in the national interest, but research indicates that the focus on health and wellness is diminishing.

19. Biotechnology and other advances will continue to increase our longevity, while there is no indication of significantly increasing birth rates, which will exacerbate the trend toward an aging and shrinking workforce.

Reasons Why Americans 55 and Older Continue Working After Retirement

Retirement refers to voluntary or involuntary termination of regular, full-time career jobs. These are the principal reasons why older Americans want to continue working after retirement:

1. Desire for continued interesting/stimulating/challenging work to maintain cognitive skills and abilities

2. Desire to maintain self-esteem and self-fulfillment by continuing in productive activities that add value

3. Desire to retain relationships with the outside world and to remain socially connected

4. Attraction of continued part-time work, without responsibility and stress of a full-time job, to enhance satisfaction with life and overall feeling of well-being

5. Opportunity, when available, for a phased retirement program or workplace options that offer greater flexibility plus an attractive benefits package that includes healthcare coverage

6. Need for additional income to maintain a standard of living or desire to have additional income for discretionary spending

7. Recognition that, with knowledge of their increased longevity and vulnerability of their financial resources through market fluctuations, it may be necessary or desirable to generate additional savings

Alternatives to "Cliff Retirement"

In "cliff retirement," people withdraw completely from regular full-time employment with the expectation of not working further. This has been the traditional approach for most people during previous years, but there has been an increasing need to re-think this approach for the following reasons:

- Demographic change has added almost 30 years to average lifespan during the 20th century; people are not only living longer but also in better health.

- There has been a major shift over the last 30 years so that employment in the U.S. is now predominantly in services rather than manufacturing; the emphasis today is more on knowledge workers than physical labor, which means that more people are in good physical condition and may wish to work beyond the traditional retirement age.

- Nationwide studies conducted among HR directors demonstrate that workers 55 and older compare very favorably with younger ones as to their overall skills and abilities, absenteeism and turnover, dedication and commitment to work, and reliability and dependability.

- All industrialized countries are confronted with an aging and shrinking workforce, with labor shortages projected for the future in these countries.

- All of the industrialized countries are confronted with the dilemma of how to reform social programs that are financially unsustainable.

- Many people 55 and older want to continue working, preferably on a part-time basis, for a variety of reasons: need or desire for additional income, satisfaction and self-esteem from continuing to add value, opportunity for ongoing intellectual stimulus, and desire to remain socially connected.

In the U.S., there is a growing trend to provide phased retirement programs and a range of flexible workplace options for older workers where they are ready and qualified to continue in productive activities. These options include:

- Reduced working hours
- Reduced working days
- Flexible working times that may be variable
- Seasonal work
- Job sharing
- Telecommuting (i.e., working from home with telecommunication connections)
- Different work assignments (e.g., mentoring or training younger workers, a new functional or business area)
- Project assignments

Another approach is for retiring workers to take "bridge jobs" that represent a way to phase down from full-time work rather than to phase out completely.

Companies are beginning to revise their employment policies and practices so that they can utilize the talents and capabilities of older workers to a greater degree. This includes the following:

- Provide more training programs for older workers to maintain or enhance their skills and abilities
- Include a segment on the management of older workers in diversity training programs for managers
- Provide phased retirement and a range of flexible workplace options
- Revise pension plans to eliminate penalties or disincentives for extended working careers
- Offer employee benefits, particularly including healthcare coverage
- Provide a retention bonus payable after a fixed additional period
- Provide life management planning guidance for workers as they approach retirement age

There is no question that demographic change will precipitate major revisions in a number of areas:

1. Change the prevalent thinking about aging and retirement
2. Substantially increase the utilization of workers 55+ by employers through the adoption of more flexible workplace policies and practices
3. Revise public policies and laws to encourage employers to utilize older workers more effectively
4. Restructure public policies, laws, and social programs to encourage, and even provide an incentive for, older people to work for longer periods of time
5. Change the retirement age under social programs to reflect the realities of demographic change

Mission Statement

The mission of the Center for Productive Longevity is to stimulate the substantially increased utilization of workers 55 and older who have terminated regular career jobs and are ready and qualified to continue in productive activities. This book is published in furtherance of the mission statement.

The book may be ordered from:
Center for Productive Longevity
4770 Baseline Road, Suite 210
Boulder, Colorado 80303
center@ctrpl.org

The Center for Productive Longevity (CPL) is a 501 (c)(3) non-profit created and funded by Human Resource Services, Inc. CPL will receive all proceeds from the sale of this book.